EXPOSED:

I Will Not Be Ashamed

Rosemary Worthy-Washington

i

"Rosemary Washington's memoir of her journey--from fire to healing, from rejection to self-acceptance, from despair to faith--is a powerful narrative of transcending courage. The reader cannot escape the depth and width of her suffering, nor can he or she escape the redemption that awaits them in her stirring story of a growing and all-encompassing faith.

Exposed is required reading for anyone who seeks tough, grounded inspiration to overcome the challenges and heavy odds of major trauma and its physical, emotional , and yes social effects.

This is a beautiful book written by a beautiful person who wants to help others become the enduring beautiful flowers of their own lives, heedless of the storm and blight that comes their way. Reading her book is a perspective changing experience that will last a lifetime."

Samuel V. Wilson, Jr.
Lt. Col. U. S. Army (Retired)

"There are not many books that can grab your attention and not let you go the way this one has. This is an amazing autobiographical account of an experience that almost none of us will ever live through to tell. Rosemary places you in the center of a story she has lived through and leaves the reader beyond amazed with an indescribable tale of triumph."

Casey Dougherty
Accountant

Written by Rosemary Worthy-Washington

Edition 2015

Copyright 2015 by Rosemary Worthy-Washington

Rosemary Worthy-Washington
ExposedIAmNotAshamed@gmail.com

Unless otherwise noted, all scripture references are from the King James Version of the Bible.

Contributors:

Back Cover Photography: Photo Illusions -
http://photoillusionscs.wix.com/photoillusions

Editing & Formatting: Lorraine Castle –
Castle Virtual Solutions LLC
http://www.castlevirtualsolutions.com/

ISBN-13: 978-0-692-51966-0
ISBN-10: 0692519661

15 16 17 18 19 RW 10 9 8 7 6 5 4 3 2 1

To my grandchildren, Neva Rose, the (my) entertainer, Noah, the (my) comforter, who both call me affectionately Grandmommie, Grandmother, and Mom. It is my prayer that when you both are mature enough to read my book, you'll be strengthened in your faith for GOD.

To my fellow burn survivors who know the unbearable pain of wound cleaning, disappointment of reconstruction surgery and rejection from society, my prayer is that this book will strengthen and encourage you to persevere and to love yourself.

To the many people who have suffered a traumatic experience and have lost their independence, may this book inspire you to press on until you overcome every obstacle.

Know this:

Proverbs 17:22 KJV "A merry heart doeth good [like] a medicine: but a broken spirit drieth the bones."

Proverbs 17:22 NIV "A cheerful heart is good medicine, but a crushed spirit dries up the bones."

Proverbs 17:22 NLT "A cheerful heart is good medicine, but a broken spirit saps a person's strength."

My prayer for you is, "No matter what you are going through, find something funny to make you laugh. It will make you feel good!"

Contents

It Happened to Me

I have lived for twenty-nine years with facial scars, one eye, no ear lobes, reconstructed nose, scars on my body, public and private challenges of a person with traumatic burns. I have lived longer with my burned face and scars than without them. I now know this face better than my born face, even though I have had a progression of faces that have led to my present face.

The automobile I was driving was a Renault Alliance. My car was brutally struck by a church passenger van. My car hit a tree, and exploded throwing me from the car. I was on fire. The driver of the van died at the accident scene. A deadly accident caused my life to be forever changed and challenged. I would endure unbelievable struggles and mind shattering experiences. I know God kept me alive for He always has a plan for our lives.

I would never know what I looked like when I was brought into the hospital from the accident scene. I would never see what my family saw at various times during my hospital stay. There were photos taken for the legal case. These photos gave me insight of how horrific that day had been. I did see photos of the early days with my face bandaged. I know it's me, but it's unbelievable how my face looks. My skin reminds me of a fried hot dog. I cannot imagine the pain my loved ones experienced when they saw me. I was told there were tubes everywhere on my body. My family said they were told by the doctors I may not live. My loved ones and friends were devastated with that information. I cry every time I think of or hear the account of that day given to me by family members. It was me o' Lord in need of

1

prayer. My family would need prayers to sustain them for the months and years ahead.

The years ahead would bring surgeries, divorce, financial problems, emotional issues and fear.

I spent three months in the burn unit. While in the burn unit, I would have many surgeries, skin grafts, and the removal of my left eye. I was on Morphine and Demerol for unbearable pain. Every four hours I was given a shot. I was on pain meds for months at a time; therefore, I had to be weaned off. I would pretend to be in pain at night so I could acquire pain meds from resident student doctors. They were sympathetic because of my facial injury. Pain meds, television and hospital chocolate cake was my life. I wanted to be high from the meds. I felt good when on drugs. I faked the need for so long that I was referred to a pain specialist. After that, I stopped the lying about having pain. I knew it was time to face my reality. I asked myself how to face my reality. One moment at a time was how I would deal with my new life. Lord, help me please!

After three months in the burn unit, I still had not seen my face. I remember a time when my two siblings came to visit me. Sadly, my brother said to me, "Rose you are messed up." My brother, James, used the "f" word. My sister, Re, short for Marie her middle name, first name Anna, chimed in and said,

"That's right Rose."

James said, "Rose you can't go outside."

I recall on several occasions when I had gone home, my mother would say to me, "I wish you were blind in both eyes so you would not have to see how your face looks." I was never able to understand that statement as I tried many times to process it, make sense of it. But, I believe Mommy meant well.

2

My thoughts were it couldn't be that bad. I knew then that I was in for a battle, a battle for my life. I recall my brother saying, "Don't let her see her face." When I saw my face, it frightened me, but instantly I said, "Oh the doctors, they can fix this. They put men on the moon, built great buildings and all doctors of course, were brilliant, and could easily give me a face."

I was told if I learned to walk, I could go home. I wanted to go home. First thing I had to do was tell my family to bring up photos of how I used to look before the accident; the doctors would need photos to work from. I spoke to my doctor and told him I was getting the photos and he said that I would not look like I used to. I said ok. So then, I began to look for photos of beautiful black women in magazines. I found several pictures of black women, I was sad I could not look like I used to but happy to know I can be pretty.

This experience would teach me that professional people will tell you enough information to keep you hopeful or until you mature enough to handle the truth. I acquired photos from magazines with hope. I was not ready to hear the report that it would take many surgeries and years before I could have a face, and it would not be normal.

My thoughts went to God. I thought, "What kind of mess am I in? What has happened to me that a doctor can't fix my face?" Again, I remembered being taught about Jesus and God in my youth. I knew with God, there was hope for my life. But was this hope going to be enough? My experiences with God were limited. What would Mommy and my husband be able to do?

I remember when my daddy died and I asked God to please let him in Heaven. My daddy expressed little about his faith. When I was a teenager daddy came to church one day intoxicated; high off liquor. Daddy sat in the pew pretending to know the songs and nodding his head to the beat of the piano. When offering time came, he walked around with his Philly black man stroll. He stood by the offering table, pulled out some ones and put a one-dollar bill in the plate. We laughed about daddy and the dollar so hard. Family members say if daddy was alive, he would have taken care of me and people would not have hurt me. I was daddy's girl. Our birthdays are four days apart.

My brother and sister's conversation in the hospital was making sense to me now. It was making scary sense. My sister and brother seemed to be without hope for me. Then I realized that my husband and mother did not have hope either. The doctor said my face would be better in the future. I said to myself, "Rose this is tragic and traumatic."

I could not recall the accident so I was not traumatized by it. My traumatization would come from the loss of my face, surgery, recovery and rejection. My injuries included broken legs, a concussion, scalp burned, nose burned, I had a gap in my teeth but it was now gone with the loss of a tooth. I could not walk. My face was unrecognizable. There was pain from my right foot with an ulcer so deep the bandages were changed daily. I had scars all over my skin. Scars the doctors made in grafting skin to cover wounds that were without skin. My left eye had been removed so I would not get an infection in my brain and I have no eyelids, no eyebrows, and only a few eyelashes on my right eye.

I lay in my bed unable to move my legs, and I hear yelling, "Oh no!" It's (Link) my then husband and the doctor. Link said, "You are not going to take her eye!"

Am I hearing this, or am I drugged off the Demerol? Link comes in and says, "They are going to take your eye because it was burned so bad that it has an infection and it will travel to your brain." My thought was, "Maybe they would not have to take it if you were not yelling at the doctor." The doctor probably thinks, "Oh I will show this guy. His wife is messed up anyway."

Besides, the doctor was white. Did he care about my husband or me? My thoughts were the doctors are probably experimenting on me, removing my eye will not matter.

4

I remember the day they took me down to remove my eye. I didn't know until I was in the room. I was drugged. I knew the eye was bad I saw it protruding from under the eyelid. My brother told the nurses, "Make sure she doesn't see her face." I was so drugged, I heard James say, "Didn't I tell you not to let her see her face?" He was talking to a nurse. I think I passed out after I saw it. If I didn't, the recall of it makes me think I did. My eye was monstrous looking.

All this was happening to me, I really thought I was dreaming, I thought I would one day wake up and my face would be back. I knew it was not a dream but something inside of me was saying this couldn't last for the rest of my life. I needed to be free from this situation.

Coming Home, Am I Dreaming

I spent five months and two weeks in St. Agnes Hospital. I spent three of those months in the burn unit under critical conditions. Today I was going home. It was a dream come true for me, but yet it felt like I was in a dream. I was not going to the home where I had lived before the accident with my husband and our daughter. My family had arranged for me to stay at my mother's home. Later I would find the reason I would stay at my mother's was because my then husband would be at work. I was scared. I didn't know what awaited me. I was afraid to think of a future at this point.

As I was getting into my mother's car, she told me to get in the back. I thought that was odd. I am the patient, the one who had been hurt; shouldn't I sit in the front? I had not been outside for months even though it felt like years. I sat in the back. It was quiet; no conversation between my family.

I was wearing a facial mask called a "job." It fit skin-tight with six holes, two holes for two eyes, one hole for my nose, a hole for my mouth and two ears. I had no ear lobes for those two holes. I had to wear a white plastic eyecup over what was once my left eye. Behind that white plastic cup was a cavity of flesh with no upper or lower eyelid. I had no nose for the mask, only two holes where nostrils used to be. I wore a skin-tight body job; the facial and the body job had to be worn for 23 hours a day. The objective was to keep the keloid scarring at a minimum. My right foot was bandaged to cover a hole; an ulcer in the location where a heel used to be.

I began to think to myself, "They have me sitting in the back of the car for my comfort." My mom turned on the radio, Whitney

7

Houston was singing the *Greatest Love of All*. The words penetrated to a part of my being I did not know even existed. I had heard this song by George Benson and Whitney many times, but this day the piercing of my spiritual being was touched with intensity. Now, I know it was my God telling me to prepare to learn to love and know me. Many times through my suffering, I placed others before myself. It would take much heartbreak before I learned to love me.

We arrived at my mother's house and immediately I was shown my sleeping area. I had returned to the home where all my dreams had started. The walls were still painted green and woodwork that was painted by me when I was a teenager was still black. The paint was peeling off the walls. There were no curtains at the window; just blinds. There was a comfort in knowing that Mommy was there, but I wanted to be at my own home where there were curtains and no chipped paint. I asked myself, "Will I be alright here after being gone for eight years?" I had changed after being gone, but Mommy would help me recover and I would be independent again.

My preparation for my going home was led by a social worker who scheduled a family meeting at the hospital. My husband, mother, grandmother, aunt, siblings and other family members were all there. The social worker spoke about my physical and emotional caring. I was dazed. Am I dreaming this moment? What has happened? I know an accident caused burns to my face and body. I see here that more had happened then just my accident. My life change would affect every one of my family members that love me. I would hear conversations from family members about what to do with Rose.

First Family Member: "We may have to put her away."

Second Family Member: "Yes, I guess so."

First Family Member: "There is no way she can look at herself every day and be all right in her mind. She was too pretty."

I knew I had to be smart, act smart and make no trouble because I did not want to be separated from my seven-year-old daughter. I was beginning to recognize that I am going through Hell. In my thoughts, I was living as if I were not injured or faceless. My mind was not lining up with my reality. I wanted my life back, but it was not coming. The reaction from the people around me was signaling me to wake up from this sleep state. I was being treated like a relative that had been gone for years and returned home without anything to contribute, money, food, etc. I must make this clear. I was fed good food, I had a TV and I could sit on the porch. What was missing was independence; I was being watched and treated as if I had a mental disability. I had no joy.

I had not realized the devastation of my accident and it would take years before I would truly know how horrible it had been. I believed I was going to be better in time. I would have a beautiful face and all would be well. My family and friends were acting as if someone had died. I found out what died, my hair, my face, an eye, a nose, lips, and areas of skin were burned. I was saying silently, "I am Rose, not a stranger." I understand the loss. It was my face. My family and I still mourn my first face.

My fellowships and relationships changed with everyone except my daughter. My daughter loved me unconditionally. My fight would be for her. Is this a dream? The people I loved the most; my husband, mother and siblings became distant, but yet, they were close. I felt they were waiting and watching for me to show signs of a mental disability.

I was released from the hospital taking antibiotics and vitamins; no pain medication or anxiety drugs. I was twenty-nine with a seven-year-old daughter who I loved and had to take care of. How was I going to do this when I was sensing strife in my family? Strife was what would contribute to my recovery. I became hopeless in my thoughts.

Whenever I saw my daughter, I began to fight in my mind. I had to change some things, but where would I begin? First thing I had to do was to have faith in God who I did not know much about. But, I believed if He would be with me, I would come through this Hell. Happy lasted for one day. Welcome Home, Rose, to my new life. I have to abide by other's rules and lifestyle. My husband and mother were the two people I relied upon for everything. They both made it a point that I had to do what they said. I had no money, no face. Hospital life and indoor living had become my life. I learned quickly that God would have to care for me and help me.

When I Wake, No More Fear

Since 1986, my morning fear came from the scheduled morning surgeries. I would awaken with anxiety and hunger. Fasting is required the night before surgery, so that's why I was hungry. I hope the anesthesiologist gives me an injection to calm my anxiety. I always like to think I have no anxiety, but there is always concern. I hope the nurse has a surgical cap for my head to cover my scars on my scalp. I hated the time when I was being rolled to the OR (operating room) and my scalp was exposed. The closer you get to the OR, the temperature changes; it gets cold. It smells sterile. I love the smell of the OR. I am offered a blanket and I say yes, and ask for two. When no one asks me, I have to request a blanket or I will be frozen stiff.

I must be as comfortable as I can be so I am aware of the goings on. They repeatedly ask me my name and my birth date. I must be aware that I go into the right room and wait for my doctor. I felt hideous, during the times of surgery when I had no eye lids, no eyebrows, no nose, no ear lobes and my mouth could not open wide enough to bite a hot dog. I was embarrassed to be me during those times. I wanted everyone to know that I used to be pretty. I knew how necessary it was for me to have the surgeries of reconstruction although there were many uncomfortable things that must be endured.

One thing I became good at was telling the anesthesiologist and OR staff; please don't put me to sleep until my doctor was there. The great thing was I would have the same surgical team for many of my surgeries. I would learn that the doctors and team saw me as a person who needed surgery to restore what was burned. They did not care what I looked like. They were there only to help me. The surgical team would talk to me and ask me questions about my life before the accident. The team recognized that I was a person. Unfortunately, outside of the hospital I was feeling less than a person.

There were times I had infections, surgeries did not work, and recovery from some surgeries could range from two days to two months. What medications would I need after surgery? I know I will need pain medication. Will the doctor prescribe enough? All these things caused me anxiety, but they had to be dealt with. I did not want to forget anything because after surgery my state of mind would be foggy from the anesthesia. I would share my concerns with whoever came to surgery with me or who would come to the hospital later. I had so many surgeries that I could go alone and a relative would come during the procedure or after.

Every day I seemed to awaken with fear. I always expected something would happen. Practically all the members in our family would say, "We are just a hard luck family." I am a witness to tragedy, not just mine, but in my family. I understand that if I don't get rid of my worries before bedtime I will have them in the morning.

I have always had fear when I wake up. My daddy would come home late at night drunk. The yelling and cursing between him and my mother was typically weekends starting on Friday and ending on Sunday night and holidays. Unfortunate situations would always occur early in the morning, "something has happened." Someone has died, or someone has beaten his wife, someone went to jail, someone was very sick and/or someone killed somebody.

Late at night, we were all in bed, when about six white men dressed in black with sticks out busted in our home looking for a neighbor. They were yelling, screaming and I knew we were all going to die. I could hear my mother screaming for my father, Jimmie, Jimmie. I could see the fear in my father's eyes as they searched our three-room apartment for drugs. They left. Mommy said, "Baby they had the wrong house." I was about 7 or 8 years old.

Then there was the early morning wake up, "Your uncle, (my mother's brother) has killed your aunt." Fear had struck again. My age is seven. My cousins' (whose ages range from 7 to 2 years old) father had brutally stabbed their mother over seven times in the neck because she left his abusiveness. Everyone was afraid of him before he murdered her. I recall there were always conversations of murder amongst adults in my family during the sixties. My mother and father had to attend to the business of murder.

My siblings and I had to stay with my grandfather's brother, his wife and son. All three of them were mean people. Fear has struck again. The overnight stay was fearful. My cousin, the son, was older; he teased us and frightened us the whole time. His parents were mean; my brother, sister and I weren't allowed to talk to each other.

Then another wake up with screams and yells from my mommy, "Jimmie, who did this to you?" Daddy had been beaten up. His face and eyes were swollen. My daddy was of light skin complexion (he was called yellow), a very handsome man with a gold tooth, tall and regal looking, but drunk. (A gold tooth was a symbol of living or coming from the south.) He told my mother who beat him up. The man who did it was tough; he took my daddy's paycheck money. My mother was going to go get it and she did. How she got it, I don't know. But what I do know is when my mother gets angry, hell has arrived. Now I understand her fearlessness. Her brother was a killer, and all the adults in the family called my mother mean Bean. Bean is because she was thinly built; my daddy said she was mean, too. As her child, I could not see her mean ways. As an adult, I now see what I never wanted to be true. She's my mother, but she can be ruthless.

There was a season in my life where I kneeled to pray before I went outside. I prayed to God for endurance to withstand whatever awaited me outside. There was a season when the staring, pointing and laughing at the way I looked from the public was horrible. I had to be mindful of the time of day and the places I needed to travel. Avoiding children, teens and men was a must.

Groups of women would nudge the others to look and see me. I recall a young man, who spoke these words, "Why are you outside?" I replied, "What?" I did not know this man. He said, "With the way you look, you should get surgery for your face." "I have had surgery and I'm getting more." He said, "You need to get another doctor." I said, "I've had three." End of conversation.

This conversation has been a reminder of my brother when he visited me in the hospital. He says, "Rose everybody knows you are ****** up. So you need to stay in the house when you come home." My sister said, "Yeah that's right Rose."

I was wondering what my brother was talking about, I thought it cannot be that bad. But it was! I just could not believe it then. There are times now after all my surgeries when people avoid me because of how I look. Oh, yes, after twenty-nine years you learn. Nevertheless, I have to be mindful how others view what is good looking and what is not. I have learned that true beauty often comes with maturity and an eye to the spirit of a person.

I remember when I would come home from being outdoors and thank God that the stares and verbal abuse were gone. The more I went to God with the cares of the stares, the stronger I got where I could withstand the stupidity, ignorance and understand that the people who were abusive and laughed at me were hurting in an area in their lives. It's amazing to watch the people who were jealous of my looks before my burns and are now glad I was burned. I also find it weird for those who are not considered good looking people to avoid me and it's the good looking people who do not mind being around me. All is flesh!

My wake up time is between 4:30 am and 5 am. I immediately thank my Father in Heaven for loving me. I am thankful that I have a relationship with God. Everyday all day my life is filled with His presence and my thoughts are of His presence. God directs my day, I ask Him to make me a blessing. I ask Him for direction through my day. When I sense fear or negativity, I seek my Father for He shows me how to navigate the issues of the world. So, fear has been intercepted with knowing that I have a relationship with the one and only living God.

Hospital Occasion

I have not eaten or drank anything since midnight. I have registered for surgery and now I wait for a nurse. The nurse takes me to my assigned room to get undressed and put on a hospital gown. I am frightened. I have had surgeries numerous times and I have learned to start preparing mentally a month in advance. I prepare mentally by saying to myself daily the surgery will be successful. I shift my mind and I say to myself, "Let's get ready, Rose, because I don't want to be scared." My preparation will kick in or activate at a precise moment. My faith works precisely, just as fear would occupy my mind like a quickly moving wave at the beach. My mind and spirit join in my protection. Faith had risen for Rose.

I have many reasons to be frightened, I have evidence and experience that surgery can be successful, but there are moments when perfection is not present. I screamed from pain in my face. My scream was for my life. Instantly I heard the doctor say, "She feels this. What did you give her?" It would be months before I learned the truth of this incident or even if it had actually happened. I waited for the opportunity to find out about the pain I experienced.

My opportunity came to read my chart to see what happened at my last surgery when I was sure I screamed with pain. My memory was correct. I have learned you have to have proof when being medicated because your mind can and will play tricks with medicating drugs. The notes reported that the anesthesiologist gave me a child dosage of anesthesia. I thought, "Unbelievable! I was not hallucinating." My surgery was a success but things can happen. I have signed the forms many times saying, "I am aware that mistakes can happen and/or I can lose my life." I ask the anesthesiologist please keep me awake until my doctor comes. I have learned to ease my frightened self by seeing my doctor before being drugged. Seeing his or her face comforts me. I know my doctor will take charge of the (OR) Operating Room.

I no longer fear surgeries or death. My faith has grown in the Lord. I say these words the moment I am given a relaxation drug, "God be with me." I say it over and over in my mind and sometimes aloud. I continue saying these words in my mind when the gas mask is placed over my face. I love the feel of the gas and can feel my body transitioning into a relaxed state along with my mind. However, I am still saying, "God be with me." I awake saying, "Thank you Jesus." If I feel pain, I yell pain medicine all the while thanking Jesus that I can feel pain and ask for medication.

My belief had grown to understand that God was always with me. I have learned, and I will say I had to choose, to think, "No matter how horrible the pain is or the outcome of my face, that if I lived, God would guide me." My job is to believe that God has a peaceful outcome for me then and now. I have always been grateful for every surgery whether successful or not. I was able to obtain a variety of surgeries because I was healthy, young enough to endure, and there was a team of doctors that were planning ways to help me. My catastrophic insurance was and continues to be a blessing in my life. God has been with me through the lonely and frustrating times that reconstructive surgery brings. I just figured after favor in areas of my life, that I did not have to fear.

My list of preparation includes who will go with me to the hospital, who will be there when I come out of surgery, and who will take me home. I have preparation lists for short procedure surgeries and hospital stay surgeries. My list for short procedures also includes, if necessary, going to the drugstore to get medication usually for pain and antibiotics. I learned quickly that healing comes fast if I am not stressed. My preparation and planning is always with healing at the forefront of this task.

Planning for surgeries in my early years of reconstruction was stressful. I spent five months and two weeks in the St. Agnes Hospital where my mother, ex-husband and sister visited daily. Taking off work for the three of them would be challenging after spending time at the hospital with me in the beginning months. I became independent quickly in my hospital traveling without a family member. I was fortunate enough to have ambulance service to take and pick me up from the hospital.

I received a million dollars' coverage for medical care concerning injuries from the auto accident. I mailed in ten dollars to the state of Pennsylvania in 1985 for my ex-husband and myself. The law was if you had a driver's license you were required to send in five dollars. I reluctantly mailed the money to the state. I did not know when I mailed ten dollars that I would benefit in a largely blessed way. I was paying for catastrophic insurance. I thought there was no way I would ever need this insurance. Approximately 325 people were given this insurance. I was one of those people. I thank God all the time for the insurance. I was able to have ambulance service because of this insurance plus over a hundred surgeries.

I was glad for surgeries. "My face would come together soon," were my thoughts. My family, my mother, ex-husband and sister were the key family members in my hospital stay and surgeries. I never heard any of them express hope. I picked up on their hopelessness. I could see them look at me and only see my face. I thought, "Did they ever know the inner me?" I wondered if they could see me. I hoped they could, but I never felt they did. I would think later that they wanted my original face and were mourning the loss. I had no time to mourn the loss of my face. My time was spent on the reconstruction of a new one with hope that it would look or resemble my original face.

My hospital stays for surgery would often last a week. I would be happy to receive the Morphine or Demerol injections. The injections worked for the pain. My body knew when I needed another shot. My body worked like a clock when it came to pain medication. I loved the Demerol. Once my pain stopped, it was party time for me. My party time in the hospital meant getting on the phone, watching television, and eating. I felt good with the Demerol in me. I had no worry and no care. I was happy in the world Demerol and I created.

My love affair with Demerol would have me seeing a pain specialist. I lied and said yes I was in pain when the wound was almost healed. The pain specialist knew I was lying. I would trick the interns, who were always scheduled late nights, that I needed a shot for pain. The interns believed me. Mostly I think they felt sad about how I looked and what I had to endure. My tricks would have a large sign posted on my chart, "Do Not Give Drugs." When I insisted, the head doctor would pay me a visit and I would receive a Percocet.

I had a close friend and we would sell valiums I received from a psychologist. In the hospital, I would receive a visit from a psychologist. It was routine. I did not need a psychologist to talk to. I wanted drugs. I told him that I would be sad sometimes. I was given a script for valium #5 or #10s. I did take them when I could not get a refill of Percocet. The valium helped me withdraw from Percocet. My close friend and I would go on Woodland Avenue and sell the valiums for fifty cents to a dollar. We only did it once. We needed some money to get a cheesesteak or hoagie.

I had visitors, friends and family, who would come to the hospital and take lotion, tissues, rubber gloves and toilet paper. I learned that everyone did not need to visit me. I would only tell a few people when I was going to have surgery. The last thing you need in the hospital is a visitor of yours taking things you need. I would soon learn that my life is serious and what was happening to me was crazy. When I say "learn" I mean learn in the sense it was time to make life-saving changes for my health and sanity. I had made the decision that only family would know when I was entering the hospital for surgery. My definition of family would change drastically.

My healing had always been a priority. I knew that some people were keeping me sick. When my daughter turned sixteen and received her junior license, change could come in regard of my support system. My support system had to change. My daughter, now a teen, and I lived together, my independence had come. My husband, mother and sister who supported me in the hospital were annoying now that I was independent of them. I had to keep my surgery dates secret. My healing would be interrupted with their negative thoughts about my daughter and me. I will speak later about relationships with my loving family.

I encountered many fears during my hospital stays and visits. I feared not waking up from surgery, I feared nurses giving me the wrong medication, I feared racism, I feared my husband and most of all I feared riding elevators. I had a phobia of elevators that started when I was eighteen years old. I was a receptionist in a factory located at 57th & Market.

One day I had to use the freight elevator to go to the lower level. On my return, the electric went out. I was not alone. There was a guy about my age who was stuck with me. The elevator stopped between the floors. I was afraid and wanted to get out. I asked the guy to lift me so I could crawl out. That very moment the owner of the company yelled at me, he said get down the electric is coming on right now. I could have been hurt.

I would find that my elevator encounters for the next few years would have me stuck again. My next experience would be at Community College of Philadelphia located on South 11th Street in Center City Philadelphia. I ran into the elevator with two other people. When the door closed, the elevator went up to the last floor, the 9th I believe. I was sweating and so scared, I began taking off my blouse. I realized I was not alone. I pushed the button to my floor and went to class.

My next elevator episode was in John Wanamaker's Department Store with my six-month old daughter, Nneka, my mother and my sister Re (Anna). I thought, "Maybe we should use the escalators instead of the elevator." We got into the elevator and it became stuck between the 9th and 10th floors. I remained calm. I pushed the red button and reported the elevator stopped moving. The voice of a man said, "We will have you out in twenty minutes." I thought, "No he did not say twenty minutes." My family was fine. They were laughing and talking and I just smiled. We all sat on the floor in the elevator. I screamed when the door opened after what seemed to be an hour, "I am never riding an elevator again."

I am part of a hospital community where the elevators are used frequently. I would ask for drugs when I knew I would be using an elevator. I know it's strange. At times, I was more frightened when I was rolled onto an elevator in a hospital bed than the surgery. I became claustrophobic. I will ride elevators when there is no alternative. My fears were a challenge but as my faith grew, I had no fear. My relationships grew with the hospital community. That includes everyone from custodial, security, social services, spiritual, nurses, technicians, specialists and doctors. My relationships grew with the people who cared about my well-being. My fear was replaced with courage and trust. I truly was blessed at St. Agnes Hospital of Philadelphia.

My experiences learned in the hospital were many. I know it's important to have someone who cares enough to fight for your wellbeing in the hospital not just for your medical care, but complete comfort. My pain medicines caused me to hallucinate many times. I recall incidents that I believe happened. My family at times ignored my complaints. I understood. The drugs caused hallucinations.

I had a nurse whose bedside manner was nasty. I asked my sister to watch this nurse's mannerisms. I am sure my sister doubted me when I said the nurse stuffed gauze in my mouth and angrily snatched the catheter from my body. Please know there is a time when the drugs wear down and wear off.

My incident occurred late at night. The nurse was hurting my mouth as she brushed my teeth. She was rough and moving hurriedly. I said nothing. She began to wash my body roughly. She pulled my arm.

I spoke and said, "You are hurting me." She said, "Shut up!" She threw my arm down after washing it. I quickly grabbed her and told her I would report her. She grabbed my other arm and I grabbed hers and said I would hurt her. I lay on my back. I cannot sit up. My nurse stuffed gauze in my mouth and snatched the catheter out. She said, "I have a date tonight and I don't have time to be wasting on you!"

I told my sister the next day. My sister said she did have a nasty attitude. It was my unfortunate experience. My point is; I watch the attitudes of people who are taking care of my family and me.

I recall when needing a dentist, how hard it was to find a dentist who did not mind doing dental work for my mouth. I was embarrassed with rejection because I could not find a good dentist. But, I was persistent and I found a great dentist who is caring and tolerant of my facial scarring.

My love for nurses, doctors, all people in health care and those who serve others are the people who I am star-struck with. I tell firefighters, police officers, sanitation workers, teachers, and preachers, "Thank you for serving and working for me." People who help and teach to make my life and your life better, I say they should be the highest paid and walk the red carpets.

The Journey of My Face

I awakened one morning at the age of ten with tiny bumps all over my face. There was no itching or redness. I would contract these tiny bumps all over my face and neck twice a year. I was getting hives and no one knew what I was allergic to. I would have a swollen nose, lips, and eyes that looked closed. My mother took me to the Mercy Douglas Hospital on Woodland Avenue, in Southwest Philadelphia. My home was five blocks from the hospital. My mother, my siblings and I walked to the hospital. I knew my mother thought my face was bad if she was taking me to the hospital, hospital costs were not affordable in our family.

I remember sitting nervously in the waiting area. My mother saw a lady she knew. The lady said, "I see James and Re, (my siblings) but where is Rose?" I was sitting right there, but I was not recognizable to her, I was not recognizable to me. My mother would tell this lady that I was sitting right there in the chair, in a corner hiding, waiting to see the doctor because my face had broken out. Broken out translated meant there were bumps and swelling. I experienced this discomfort every year. My hives got worse. The bumps would itch. My eyes would swell and form mucous until seeing was very difficult. I would have a hard time eating food. I needed a straw to drink. I even had the hives when I enlisted into the United States Army. I never found out what I was allergic to or why I contracted the hives yearly. My hives did not show up during my pregnancy at twenty-one and thereafter, no hives.

My year in the United States Army would teach me discipline and showed me things I could endure physically and mentally. My preparation for my facial change definitely was heaven-sent. My endurance in Basic Training strengthened me in the area of

25

withstanding people teasing, mocking, and not liking you. Basic Training consisted of Drill Sergeants getting in your face yelling and cursing at you for absolutely no reason. The mental exercises or games made many of the female recruits cry. My brother and husband had gone in the military before me, so I was warned that it's a head game. I knew to do whatever they said and do it well. My endurance during "Big Wac" was great. Big Wac is a weekend in the woods. Comfort was not available. Rations were distributed to last for the weekend. We slept in tents with sleeping bags. My few times attending Big Wac; it always rained the whole weekend. I was convinced the army made it rain. My experience in the army prepared a foundation of mental, physical and emotional strength.

I believe having the hives on my face was part of my journey to experience facial change; a way of preparing me for my burnt face. The facial change at 10 years old and twenty-nine were both shocking. My shock resulting from the doctors not being able to restore my face was horrifying. My hives experience taught me how to sit still. My parents would always say sit still when you were sick. I learned stillness. I learned calmness. I learned to let it heal and believe that it would. The hives taught me that they would go and come at will. I learned to journey through the process. My hives experience was creating a memory for my journey of facial difference that would last my lifetime.

My burn scars must be watched in case there are bruises. Burned skin can easily bruise and take longer to heal then normal skin. I have found that what can heal can become a wound again. I recall having surgeries where the surgeons would perform debridement on my face. Debridement is defined as "the cutting away of dead or contaminated tissue or foreign material from a wound to prevent infection." I have had many debridement surgeries that included my face, abdomen, right foot, leg, and right thigh. I suffered horrible pain having the debridement surgeries. I have had surgeries beginning January 8, 1986 thru May 10, 1999. I have had over a hundred surgeries.

I was thankful for Demerol, Morphine and Percocet. I was addicted to this medication and I had to be weaned off before leaving the hospital. The three months spent in the burn unit during my critical period, I was heavily medicated. I would stay on the regular floor for two months and two weeks. My stay on the floor was a happy move from critical care. I was transitioning in many ways physically, emotionally and my reality was creeping into my mind. Physically I was getting stronger.

I was concerned about my marriage and my daughter. I had known my husband since I was fourteen. I recalled the state of our marriage and remembered we had separated for two weeks before my accident. My daughter was seven. I hoped she was spending lots of time with my mother. My thoughts of them shook whatever comfort zone I might have thought I had. I wanted my family, my daughter and my husband. My reality of the trauma that happened was becoming clearer than I wanted to see or accept. My focus shifted to surgery. My hope out of this dilemma was having my face fixed.

I remember hearing news of Richard Pryor and Michael Jackson suffering traumatic burn injuries. Their burn injuries happened years before mine. I wondered if I had or would be receiving similar treatments. I read where Richard Pryor had whirlpool baths and surgery to remove dead tissue from his body, debridement. I spoke about myself receiving the same type surgery. I did receive the whirlpool baths. I recall always receiving an injection of Morphine or Demerol to ease the pain while removing the bandages so I could get into the whirlpool.

Michael Jackson had suffered burns to his scalp and it is easily seen in photos that captured the actual burning. I, too, suffered burns to my scalp. I would receive surgery to restore my hair in the areas where it had been burned. I had a surgery that would insert a "tissue expander" into my scalp. The tissue expander is placed in my scalp surgically. After the healing process, I was preparing myself for another traumatic experience that is intended to give me hair. I would have saline injections weekly for six months. These injections were going into the tissue expander that is now in my head. I watched my scalp grow every week. I talked to God a lot during this process.

My tissue expander had been filled to capacity with saline. I would now be scheduled for another surgery to remove the tissue expander and, hopefully, enough skin with hair would cover the burn area. I endured six months of injections, watching my head grow, uncomfortable sleeping, and it did not work. My trauma experiences were becoming a lifestyle. I cannot remember if the tissue expander surgery happened again but I know there was talk to try. I do have photos of the enlarged scalp that remind me of the Elephant Man.

I understand why Michael wore wigs after his burn to the scalp. I assume his surgery for his scalp did not work either. I was thankful that my entire scalp did not burn. I have two close girlfriends who would do my hair after the burn injury. Connie and Eileen were very caring. I am forever thankful and grateful to them. I remember a lot of fun times with Connie, my best friend, and Eileen, my God sister. My friend Connie was helpful in my confidence to drive again with one eye. I'll share that story later.

I learned to keep moving and fighting for my recovery. I saw Richard Pryor and Michael Jackson living their lives regardless of their burn injury. Richard Pryor made jokes and kept his life moving. Michael wore wigs and kept singing. I recall many days wishing that I could have had Richard Pryor and Michael Jackson's surgeons or visit California where it's been said the best surgeons were. I did inquire to my surgeons. Disappointingly, it was expressed to me that they could do no more in California than I was receiving in Pennsylvania.

I would not be defeated. I will go on with my life and conqueror my obstacles. Richard Pryor and Michael Jackson continued on with their lives. I too will continue to see where my life will lead me. I have to know that I did all I could do for me first and then others. I knew that I, Rosemary, was in need of prayer, miracles and direction from God.

How Do I Live With One Eye?

I did not have a long discussion with the doctors about the removal of my left eye. I mentioned earlier that my then husband was in a loud and yelling conversation with one of my doctors about saving my eye. I am reminded of a time when my father set the upstairs of our house on fire. I know Daddy and Mommy argued a lot, but I never knew what caused him to set fire to the house. I was about twelve years old, on my way to my grandmother's house. She lived about two blocks away from our home. My block has 16 houses. There is a playground located across the street from my old house. The playground has had two name changes. Before my teen years, it was named Johnson Playground. In my teen years, the name was changed to 48th & Woodland Avenue Recreation Center. Today the name is the same. All the children and adults in the neighborhood called it our playground. Yes. It was ours. I played in the playground beginning at the age of five. When I visit the area as an adult, I just look into the playground and see the years past. I see all the people I played with, grew with and even people I never knew.

I remember walking alongside the playground cement wall when Daddy ran towards me. My house was on a hill. As you walk down the block, the playground cement wall would get higher and higher to the height where looking into the playground would be impossible. I remember it being summer and not a hot day, but summer cool. I can smell fried chicken and hear Stevie Wonder's song *Blowin' In The Wind*. My daddy grabs me and says, "Rose, come with me." My daddy looks at me and says, "I set the house on fire." I looked at him confused. My daddy says, "Come with me and you'll be alright." I hear my mother call, "Rose!" I look back at her and say, "Daddy said he set the house on fire." My mother turns around and runs back to the house, and Daddy looks at me with a sly smile and speedily walks away. I then run back to my house and soon the fire department is there putting out a fire in my house.

I don't know how I will live with only one eye. My health is in jeopardy if the bad eye is not removed. I don't know how I will live without my father. My mother had every right to be angry and not want Daddy to live with us. My daddy was a danger. I was heartbroken when Daddy didn't come home for a long time. I knew the day had come when my eye would be removed. I was drugged but I recall fighting the drugged state in my mind with the hope of knowing what was happening to me. The fight would be one I would lose. I wanted to say goodbye to my eye. I wanted to say goodbye to a pretty eye, brown with long eyelashes. My eye had been with me for 29 years.

My brother was in the U.S. Army, We were taking him back to Fort Dix, NJ and we were lost. I went into a bar to ask for directions. I saw no one in this bar except the bartender. It was in the middle of the afternoon so the bar was well lit. A song was playing by Gene Chandler, *The Duke of Earl*. I proceeded to ask the bartender for directions. As he spoke, I looked into his eyes. They were the prettiest brown eyes I had ever seen. I knew with the removal of my eye, I would never have that effect on a man again.

I remember a man standing in white attire and a white mask that covered his mouth and nose. The man wore glasses. My next thought was I had awakened with an eye bandage on what used to be my left eye. I prepared myself for the removal of the bandage. When the bandage came off, I saw a cavity with pink flesh, without eyelids and no eye.

I wondered what my seeing would be like now. Will I be able to drive? I must protect the one eye I have. My questions led to fear. I would spend the rest of my life protecting my one eye every day. I knew I had to learn to live with one eye. Who would teach me? Whom did I know with one eye? Mr. Robinson; he lived on the block I grew up on and he still drives.

I often wondered if I could drive because I now had one eye. My friend Connie who combed my hair would often accompany me to the hospital. An ambulance with two drivers would come and take me. One of those drivers liked Connie. I decided to see if I could drive the ambulance on a particular day while Connie and the two drivers were talking. I turned the ambulance vehicle on and moved it a few feet. I was convinced that I could drive again. The drivers were yelling and Connie was laughing. Connie with her good looks and charm captured their attention, which gave me an opportunity to drive giving myself confidence. My confidence was getting stronger.

I was happy when the doctor said they were going to build eyelids for me. I knew with eyelids, I could then get a prosthetic eye. I knew slowly I was being put back together physically. My being put back together was a slow process. I had at least seven surgeries for my eyelids to be completed. My sister said, "Rose every time you go into the hospital for surgery, you always look worse than you did going in." We would laugh and know that statement was the truth. I understand what I was unable to verbalize during the many surgeries. I learned the journey, the building, the process can be painful, ugly, hard, but when it's over there is beauty in the things that were endured and overcome. I learned and received understanding after all the processes, that's how wisdom is obtained.

My car I had my accident in was a navy blue Renault. I liked the Renault because it reminded me of an old Volvo I had. My grandfather had a heart attack and he was in a hospital in Camden, New Jersey. My husband, father, mother, grandmother, and I went to see my grandfather in that Volvo. My grandfather was going to be all right and we were all happy. I was driving over the Benjamin Franklin Bridge when a police officer's car was behind me and then there was a voice coming from a microphone or bullhorn. I heard a voice saying, "Pull over. Your car is on fire." I drove quickly to an area that's just off the bridge and turned off the car. I instantly jumped out as fast as I could. We were all trying to get everyone out of the back seat. We watched the smoke in the front area of the car. The fire department came and put the fire out. The burning came from wires. My family and I were scared as we got everyone to safety. My family walked to catch public transportation and laughed about how we were trying to get my grandmother and father out the car. Because of their intoxication from drinking, it was hard for them to move quickly. The scene was funny when it was over.

The mechanic said the car wires needed to be replaced. I had the wires replaced, but the Volvo was never the same. Eventually, it was junked. My eyes would never be the same. The fire had destroyed the original skin and the rebuilding would happen but there would likely be some problems. I would never have eyelashes with the eyelids being rebuilt. My right eye, normally I say my good eye, but I will call it my great eye from now on. My great eye does not shut completely when I sleep. I have to keep it lubricated at all times. It helps with my vision and the lubrication keeps it protected. My great eye has eyelashes but they are not full eyelashes. I will never wear false eyelashes because the prevention of any possible infection is priority for my great eye.

My prosthetic eye is made very well. Most people think it's my great eye. My prosthetic eye has slight movement. The price of my prosthetic eyes were costly but worth it to me. I thank God for my catastrophic insurance, which pays at 100%. I believe my first eye was in the range of a thousand dollars. The cost for my present eye was about fifteen hundred dollars. My eyebrows were burned also. My doctor tattooed my eyebrows and it was painful. My forehead had been burned and my skin is very tight in that area. The tightness of the skin made it difficult to numb the area. I have learned to draw eyebrows or not and just wear bangs.

I learned what it is like not being able to see at all. During my hospital stay in the effort to save my great eye it was stitched closed. I had no sight for several days. I was heavily drugged during this time. I know God knew I needed to be. I recall waking up and not being able

32

to see and I yelled, "I am scared, I can't see!" I could hear a woman say, "Your eyes are sown shut." I felt her arms go around me, I said, "Don't touch me I must pray right now." I cried out to God, "God help me! I am scared. Please help me!" I cried out and I opened my eye. I yelled, "I see you!" to a white nurse. I began to name everything I saw. I saw cereal in a cup and the nurse had on pink lipstick. I said to her, "God answered my prayer." She replied, "No, you burst your stitches by crying." I replied, "However it happened does not matter, I asked and I received," and then I asked for a phone to call my mother because I wanted to see her.

I am thankful for my great eye and my prosthetic eye. I learned that God will truly show up when He knows you cannot take anymore. I could not see and I could not take anymore. My God, I thank you for coming to my rescue, always.

Reconstruction of My Nose

I wondered from the time I saw my face without a nose, "How would I get a nose again?" I had no bridge and my nostrils lie flat as a pancake on my face. I thought of myself looking like the monsters in a black and white movie, hideous and ugly. My nose would run and I had no feeling from my nose. My smelling had changed. My patience had matured. Learning to wait for reconstruction of my nose while I was enduring other painful surgeries taught me patience. My doctors had a plan. I did express my desires to my doctors but there was a process I had to follow. My patience became my friend and we would have critical conversations. My patience would say, "Don't cry and don't be sad. The building of my nose must be handled delicately so it would be done right."

The reconstruction of my nose would begin in April 1988. I had my accident in 1986. My thoughts were, "This is taking too long." My preparation of the reconstruction of my nose started with a tissue expander being placed in my upper right arm on the side of my bicep muscle. I spoke previously about a tissue expander for my scalp to transfer skin with hair to other areas of my scalp. After the insertion of the tissue expander in my right arm I would then receive saline injections to stretch the skin, duration of this procedure would be six months. I was glad when my six months were completed because now the actual work to the nose area would begin. The stretched skin from my right arm would now be attached to my face, the nostril area. My nose reconstruction was a big deal and important to my looking normal again.

My nose has always been a teaser with my siblings especially around Christmas time. I loved to watch *Rudolph the Red Nosed Reindeer* every Christmas season. I expected to be teased by my sister and brother when *Rudolph the Red Nosed Reindeer* television show came on. My nose was cute to me. My siblings laughed about it turning red at certain times. When I blew my nose or sneezed, it would turn reddish. My brother and sister would sing the Rudolph song, point at my nose and laugh. I was sad and mad when they teased me about my nose. I found it strange that I liked my nose but felt shame because of my brother and sister's teasing. I still miss my nose but I am thankful for the nose that was reconstructed. My nose is a miracle for me. I hope when you see the photo of me without my nose that you will understand why I call my nose "a miracle."

I have been asked many times before my nose was reconstructed, "Can you breathe?" "Can you smell?" My answer was always yes to both questions. Rarely would I tell people when the humidity was high, I was uncomfortable breathing. I used a humidifier when breathing was harder than usual. I was uncomfortable breathing in small rooms with little ventilation. I would keep my mouth open to breathe comfortably. My sense of smell did not work well because of my nose injury. The smell of fried chicken or fish before reconstruction was faint. My taste of food was also affected by the injury to my nose. My voice sounded nasal or congestive. I regrettably endured this uncomfortable way of living without any option or choice.

I found patience to be a virtue. My surgery on April 25, 1988 was the beginning of reconstruction for my nose. On May 9, 1988, I had my right arm attached to my face, where my nose had been located. In the month of May, I endured four reconstructive surgeries. I would endure a total of 22 surgeries for my nose. Included in the surgeries was a bone graft from my right hip to my nose on November 14, 1988. I remember the recovery for the bone removal was very painful. I needed a cane to walk. I had no regrets of the painful bone graft. I needed a cane and therapy to recover. My nose now has a bridge.

I endured many emotions from April 25, 1988 through November 1988. I was fearful and hopeful, sometimes minute-to-minute. I knew what was happening physically, but emotionally I was grieving. I was grieving the nose of my youth - where had it gone and why was it gone. I knew the answers to these questions when I disciplined myself to think critically. My Father in Heaven knows the emotional breakdown I could have had without faith. I found it unbelievable how embarrassed I would be when I discussed with family and friends my experiences of reconstruction on my nose. I was embarrassed. I was ashamed. What had I done to have such painful and unbelievable experiences in my life? I asked God to help me go through even if I don't understand why.

I received another tissue expander for my left arm to be attached to the area of my nostrils in March 1990. My monthly injections of saline to the tissue expander would go on for several months. My reconstruction for my nose would continue until 1996. The many surgeries for my nose were hopeful. I had accepted my way of life during these years. My life consisted of surgery, recovery, healing, infections, medications, doctors and hospitals.

I recall the first consultation with the doctor about my nose. The doctor asked me did I smoke. I replied yes. He said I must stop if I wanted the surgeries to work. The doctor said they would be removing veins and blood vessels from my arm that would be used for my nose. On that day, I stopped smoking forever. My breathing can sometimes be uncomfortable and periodically I wear tubes in my nose for stretching. I am thankful to God who has journeyed with me throughout many procedures. My nose is unique and the processes I went through to receive my nose have been unbelievable.

My Right Foot

I received a tissue expander in my right leg for the needed skin for a burn on my right heel. My right heel had been burned to the bone. I remember a guy saying to me, your foot looks like an elephant foot. I thought, "How rude of him." I then silently agreed to myself that it does. I thought about the pain and the urgency of the care of my right foot that of which he had no idea. I never told him. My thought was he didn't care. I knew he just wanted to swim in my pool. I will speak more about the responses of men later.

My right heel was attached to my right leg where the tissue expander stretched skin that was needed for the healing of my foot. My foot was attached and in this position for six weeks. I was in the hospital during this time. I could not get out of bed so the bedpan was my toilet. I remember during this time talking to my mother-in-law on the phone. She could sing. I loved her before I loved her son. My visits to her home were like attending a concert at the Dell in Philadelphia. I would sit in the living room and listen to her sing.

My mother-in-law's son, my ex-husband, was in the U.S. Army. I remember her encouraging me during her fight with breast cancer. I recall her saying that things were not going good. I said, "Mom, you will be fine." I believed that. My mother-in-law was a great inspiration for me. She said, "No, baby." I cried and said, "Mom I need and love you." My mother-in-law said when one door closes another will open. The door that would open was always there. I had to open the door and accept God in my life. Her love has not been replaced to this date. My mother-in-law passed. I know I was blessed. Many women don't get great mothers-in-law.

I received the skin on my right heel. I experienced many years of bandages on my heel after surgery. My heel never completely closed. In 2005, I read a book called *Healed Without Scars*, by Bishop David G. Evans. I was inspired and my faith strengthened by reading this book. I decided every time I thought of my heel, I would lay hands on it and say these words, "By His stripes, I am healed." I did this for several months. I prayed and saw the dime-sized hole drain fluid daily. I believed in spite of what I was seeing.

I purchased a mirrored vanity from an Amex catalogue for one thousand dollars. My perfumes and jewelry were kept on the mirrored vanity. I lay in my bed during evening hours and suddenly I heard a crackling, breaking sound. It was a strange sound. I got up, looked around to see where this sound was coming from and as I stood still, I saw the crack in the mirrored vanity. I wondered how and why the vanity cracked. The room temperature was neither extremely cold nor hot. I was amazed to see the crack in the mirror was familiar in its shape. I was led to look at the hole in my foot. My hole was closed and no fluid present. The scar on my foot is the shape of the crack on the mirrored vanity. I thanked God immediately for my heel being closed. I was bewildered about the shape of the crack in the mirror. This is God's doing. I told myself I would not share this happening. I needed to know I was secure in what I was experiencing. My God had answered my prayers after laying hands on my foot and proclaiming by His stripes I am healed.

I realized that this miraculous event would not be received by some. I would praise and look at my heel throughout the day every day. I had a doctor tell me that the hole would never close. My routine visits to this doctor always started with debridement. The hole always got bigger on those visits. I stopped letting this doctor treat me, he was a podiatrist. I don't think he was good in helping with burn ulcers.

I am grateful and will always be happy for the healing and reconstruction of my burn injuries. I had to work hard at not being ashamed of my burn scars. I learned that change isn't change until it's changed. I am referring to how I had to grow through the processes of my acceptance of my physical self. My challenges would always come by a remark positive or negative by someone in regard to my scars.

I was ashamed to go without stockings or socks. Today I can feel like an alien when it comes to my right foot being exposed. I am always watching closely when receiving a pedicure and a foot treatment. I mentioned earlier about the guy who said I had an elephant looking foot. As grateful as I am for the healing of the hole in my foot, I always remember how I felt when I agreed silently. My critical thinking had to defend this negative statement. My foot was burned severely and saved with grafted skin. I am thankful. Had the burn been worse, I would have had no foot to compare to an elephant. I will not be ashamed.

My memories of the days when I had to wear a specially made shoe were hopeless days. I recall years of hoping to be able to wear regular shoes. I would finally be able to wear sneakers. I could not wear any brand sneakers. I wore New Balance sneakers when the make was not stylish as they are today. I had to have special inserts made for my sneakers and my shoes when I graduated to shoes. My doctor advised me to switch shoes daily. It gave me an advantage of watching my foot for breakage of my thin-skinned foot.

My celebration of my foot would be a half marathon that I would run in 1999 for Jefferson Hospital of Philadelphia. I prepared and bandaged my foot with the hole. I ran conscious of sparing my heel not to hit the street or concrete. I recently ran another half marathon in April 2015 with the heel closed. I bandaged and prepared my heel. I maintained to run without hitting my heel on hard ground. I praise God every time I run whether it's a marathon or not. My right foot has had a few surgeries to save it from being amputated. My strut with my head held high when I wear high heels is me walking with praise to my God.

Me and the Elephant Man

I decided to watch the movie titled *"The Elephant Man."* I've always been amazed how a revelation differs after watching the same movie twice after years have passed. When I first saw *"The Elephant Man,"* I had not had my accident and I was younger. My view of the movie then was one of sadness for the man with the messed up face. Now that I am older and have experience in the area of a messed up face I would not use that description anymore. I would say he has a disease, injury and/or a situation that is traumatic.

I watch the movie and I know what it feels like to be treated horribly because of your face. I have felt many times, there is nothing I can say or do to stop evil responses to how I look. The Elephant man would respond by being calm and saying nothing. I thought of him going inside himself as I have done many times when people stare. In my mind I say, "It's all right. They do not understand why you look the way you do and they are unaware that you are hurting by their lack of compassion and understanding." Jesus said on the cross, "Forgive them for they know not what they do."

I imagine the Elephant man learned to be calm from daily reading the bible. In the movie, you see him reading his bible often while in his room alone. I have learned from many of my hardest times being quiet, calm and still comes from me meditating on the presence of God in my life. I find God present when there are no physical signs of His presence, when everything is wrong, but yet, I know now that He is with me. There is a peace when you surrender to His presence, not to the madness.

I cried and still cry because of being treated badly and sometimes just because I am stared upon. I can cry when I have been blessed by someone who stared and I know that my presence has been a blessing of hope to them. Rarely was the Elephant man treated kind in public, but when surrounded by people who were compassionate, he received kindness and praise. The Elephant man cried a great deal.

I can say whenever I am treated kind by people I have a sense that the Lord is blessing them, instantly right in my presence. I believe God does bless those who bless people who are usually treated with reluctance and as though they are not normal. I must add when people treat me regular without any signs of reluctance to my scars, I am grateful to God for them and I pray for them.

I remember the times I was told that my face would never be normal looking. I say "times" because more than a few times this conversation was needed to convince me that a normal face was not going to happen. In the movie, the Elephant man asks the doctor could he cure him of the disease that caused his facial abnormality, the doctor responded no, we can only care for you and keep you comfortable. I had no disease but the facial deformity was there. I had no nose, no eye or eyelids. I, too, look hideous and I felt hopeless. I didn't want to think about my face not being able to look normal, but it was all I thought about. Even when I didn't think about it, it was parked in my mind. My next question was, "Can I have a normal looking face?" The answer from the doctors, "We will try."

Many years were spent trying to convince myself that I would never be pretty. I noticed at times, I felt pretty in my mind. Where were these thoughts coming from? They were coming and I liked the way I was feeling. I have learned what you think about yourself will show up on the outside and speak out of your mouth. I continually learn that when I love myself, the best of me comes forth. I have struggles fighting for me because many people have said negative things about my look and I fought not to believe them, but when you see deformity on you, it's a rough fight. I tell you God was in my mind. God was speaking to me. It will be better was in my spirit. I

44

know God was talking about my life, not just my face. My life was in need of reconstruction along with my face.

I watch the Elephant man's journey, his relationships with people, his triumphs and his pain and I see the similarities with having a deformed face. I am filled with his joys, his grief and now he lies down with his bible in his hand and dies.

I am filled with my joy knowing that knowing God will pay off in my life. I am thankful for the uniqueness of my life. God came that we can live life abundantly. Unlike the Elephant man, my face was reconstructed, I have had lots of protection. I have people who love me. I live in an era where there is information about rare diseases and I am grateful to be living in this era. I will remember the most important similarity that I have with the Elephant man and that is seeking God daily for strength to endure the experiences in my life journey.

Places I Find Comfort

I was first introduced to trauma at the age of seven. I have always found funerals a place of comfort. I attended a church where I volunteered as the Funeral Coordinator. I would meet with the families and make arrangements for their loved ones. On the day of the funeral, I would make sure the family was comfortable and that everything went as scheduled. Coordinating funerals blessed me greatly. I helped people during a sad time in their lives. The families never seemed to care how I looked. Well, no one complained or showed discomfort in my presence. I had found my lane. I also joined the Hospital Ministry and the Nursing Home Ministry. I was being a blessing and getting blessed in these ministries. I learned most times when people are at their saddest and weakest, how I looked did or does not matter. I know how I look now and have photos to remind me of my facial progress. I say these things because many people have said it's not how I look. I have been told that some people stare because they marvel at my strength and may wonder about what happened. I do not deny those reasons. I have found them to be true. I also have seen and heard people respond negatively.

I became good at accepting death, murder, sickness and disappointment in my youth. My mother's brother killed his wife by stabbing her and cutting her throat. I was seven when this happened. My mother took us to the apartment where he killed her. I remember the smeared blood circle in the middle of the floor on a linoleum rug. We also went to the funeral parlor where my aunt laid in a soft pink gown, she was beautiful. I was sad. Mommy looked closely around her neck where she looked for the scars on her neck and throat. I recall trying to see by standing on my tip toes. Mommy said, "Get back."

My mother said, "There it is," referencing the scar. She was hurt, sad and crying. She loved her sister-in-law. They were close.

We would visit my uncle in prison for the next seven years. Rahway Prison, I hated the name of the prison but liked the car ride to the prison. Our family did not travel many places. If police were near, my grandfather or father would say, "Keep your head straight. Don't look back." They feared the police and now I understand why. Now fifty years later I still won't look back if there is a police presence. Now I fear the police and tell my grandchildren don't look back. Packing a lunch and food for my uncle was a big deal. When we arrived, there would be a picnic if it was summer, if it was winter we would be indoors. I hated being indoors. I can never do prison ministry because I don't like being locked in any place where I need someone to let me out.

My uncle was locked up and I was angry about that. I was seven and he was a murderer, but I loved him. When I became an adult, then I pitied him. As an adult, I knew he was not rehabilitated after seven years. I knew he had mental issues. He had no remorse. My uncle told me he would do it again, He was still angry. I was told that because she left him, he killed her. I recalled he beat her often. Everyone feared him except my mother.

I learned early in my youth that you attend funerals to support the living family members. There is a culture that exists when people die. Adult members of my family would take food and cases of soda to the grieving family. I remember hearing adults speak about the price of burying a loved one and whether there was a life insurance policy. The insurance man came every Saturday and my mother would say I don't have $5.00 to pay the insurance man and instruct us to get away from the door. I never knew that $5.00 could do so much. I paid the state of Pennsylvania $5.00 in 1985 for catastrophic insurance that would pay a million dollars' coverage if I were injured in an automobile accident. I received that million-dollar coverage for my medical injuries. My lawsuit paid me two million dollars. I will speak more about my finances later.

My grandmother always paid her policy on time. I suppose because my grandparents were older, the need to keep the policy current was important. The casket and the amount of flowers at a funeral was an indication if the family had received enough money from the policy or whether they kept the money for other reasons. In my youth going to a funeral meant a few things. During the service, we would possibly see people screaming, crying for their loved ones and sometimes even fighting. Eating at the repast was usually a jubilant time of socializing. Occasionally if a man died, he had outside children that no one knew about and sometimes another wife. It amazes me the things we heard as children and how in adulthood you understand these unfortunate situations that may happen. My thoughts as a woman of God is with the deceased, I pray they transitioned in the presence of God.

Going to funerals would be a time to reunite with people. In my teens and twenties death was a regular visitor. The young black men in my neighborhood were shooting each other because of gang affiliation. Young people were overdosing from drugs. Older people would die in their sleep. Rarely would you hear someone dying from a disease. Usually high blood pressure, strokes and heart attacks would be the standard cause of death in the black family. So, if it was not the youth dying, it was our parents and grandparents. Funerals were frequent in my young life. Being at a funeral in my youth did not upset me. Attending funerals is a natural occasion for me. I did know of people in my youth who hated funerals.

Wanting and acting tough with the "I don't care attitude" became my defense against the tragedies of life. My thoughts were this is how it would always be, hard times. This was life. I learned to find acceptance and comfort in the places of death, sickness and hard times.

My mother took my siblings and me to church. Train up a child is truth. [Pro 22:6 KJV] "Train up a child in the way he should go: and when he is old, he will not depart from it." There was hope for my life.

I accepted Christ at seven. I believed that there was a God and now He was mine. I knew no more about the gospel at the moment, but I was happy, I had a joy, and there was a God who was strong and mighty to take care of me.

I am reminded that I am not my body when I attend funerals. There is a comfort in knowing that this body is not me. I am an immaterial being. I am a spiritual being having natural experiences as I am journeying my way back to my Father in Heaven. Funerals are a celebration of a life that was. Funerals are a reminder that God houses spiritual beings in a temporary vessel called a body with flesh, bones, organs and blood. The body was made from dirt and God made man.

We are reminded in sickness and death how we are sojourners. We must remember that our spiritual being is freed from the vessel at death and is now in the presence of God.[2Cor5:6] "Therefore we are always confident, knowing that, whilst we are at home in the body, we are absent from the Lord: 7(for we walk by faith, not by sight:) 8we are confident, I say, and willing rather to be absent from the body and to be present with the Lord."

A family crisis triggered my attention to my emotional, mental and physical health. I had been neglecting the whole me. I realized I was trying to help everyone else have a better life. I insisted that they do so. I am the oldest of my siblings and I always tried to make sure their lives, my mother and grandparents were well.

I went to God confused about the family crisis. My conversation with God:

Me: God aren't I supposed to help everyone in my family?
God: Rose, give the message and I handle the rest.
Me: (Total silence.)
God: I direct the journey of all people.
My thoughts: Have I honored God in taking care of myself in every area of my life?

My retrospect of myself revealed the areas where I was failing in my finances, my health, my business, and my relationship with God. I realized I had no peace and no comfort. I knew it was time to shut all the nonsense out of my life.

I found myself in a place where I was angry at myself. There was no comfort. I felt I had cheated myself out of an honest mourning for the loss of my physical and sudden life change. I had not gone through a process of mourning led by me for me. I realized that all of these years had been spent trying to convince everyone that I could handle this change in my life, accepting different faces.

I needed to spend time with each scar, each injury, each memory, each failure, each accomplishment and each rejection. I had to know this had not been a dream I've been living. I kept journals and photos, which helped me greatly. I knew this mourning process meant, "no outsiders allowed." I've kept negativity away from me, including the media.

If you have not lost your face, you would not be allowed into my space. If your relationship with God was abnormal to the world, you were allowed into my space. I knew I was and am a spiritual being having a human experience. I desired these two categories of people close to me during the mourning of me. I will add, it was limited.

I knew there would be many who would say I had lost my mind, shutting everybody out. My life and the love of me had to come before everything and everybody. I realized no one person can experience my journey, neither I theirs. I learned that my relationship with God is my life. No one comes before God. Who can do what He can? No one!

I had to come face to face with my face and acknowledge the spiritual being that God said I am. Knowing my spiritual being made my human being a better human. I found my mourning time to be a time of rising. Spending time with God rose me up and gave me clarity into who I am and that I belong to Him.

My mourning time about my physical and spiritual transition has been completed to my satisfaction. I no longer work at convincing people I am sane or I can handle the physical change. I will dwell in the spiritual place of the Lord forever.

There's a song titled "*Without You*" by Denita Gibbs. She sings how we cannot live without our Father in Heaven. She sings that we can't move, can't breathe, can't live without the Lord, no other help, and that we need Him everywhere we are. Denita Gibbs sings the words. I agree that, "without God, I can't live without Him."

Pretty Ugly

I watched a family movie with my grandchildren. My granddaughter Neva Rose is five and my grandson Noah is eleven. I liked the movie; it is called *Blended*. The movie is about two families that travel to Africa. The movie had a man who played an African salesman; his teeth were buck-teeth. My granddaughter, grandson and I share in a conversation on facial looks.

> Granddaughter: That man is ugly.
> Me: Don't say things like that; it's not nice.
> Granddaughter: But he is.
> Me: People call me ugly; I know you don't want anyone to say that about me.
> Grandson: But you had an accident.
> Me: Everyone doesn't know that or care that I had an accident.

Beauty defined in Webster's dictionary is, "1. The quality attributed to whatever pleases or satisfies the senses or mind, as by line, color, form, textured, proportion, rhythmic motion, tone, etc., or by behavior, attitude, etc., 2. A thing having this quality 3. Good looks 4. A very good-looking woman 5. Any very attractive feature."

I am aware that my looks are defined in a positive way. I have pleased and satisfied someone's senses. I am so grateful for two clichés, "beauty is in the eye of the beholder" and "beauty is only skin deep." My physical looks have been classified by others in our environment and are not favorable by the majority, "What should I do? How do I handle unfavorable responses?"

I used Webster's to define beauty. This is how it defines ugly; "1. Unpleasing to look at; aesthetically offensive or unattractive;

unsightly 2. Bad, vile, repulsive, offensive, objectionable, 3. Threatening; ominous 4. [Informal] ill-tempered cross; an ugly person or thing."

My looks are defined in this definition in a negative and hurtful way. I understand the definition.

I asked the question, "What should I do? How do I handle unfavorable responses?" I am thankful for the word of God. Part of a scripture that I use in my thinking is from Proverbs 23:7 (KJV). "For as he thinketh in his heart, so [is] he:" I think in my heart of the many compliments I've received from my family. They always said I was cute, pretty, looked like my mother and father. I recall the male relationships and their favorable compliments. I will speak more on male relationships. My thinking came from the media whether it was favorable or not. I knew what pretty should look like in the physical sense according to our culture in the United States. My answer to what I should do is to think on those favorable compliments and statements. I had to find a way to respond to the negativity and the answer is simple. Do not respond when responding is not helpful in the situation. I discovered that it was up to me when to respond.

After knowing the meaning of beauty and ugly, I was able to ask myself the hard questions. I knew just thinking of the compliments of others would not be enough to keep me from being depressed. I had to ask myself the hard raw questions and know that regardless of my answers, I would still love me. My questions to myself were, "Do I like how I look?" No. I do not like how I look. "Do I understand why I look this way?" Yes. I understand why I look this way. My facial change and scars are the results of the fiery auto crash and the outcome of surgeries. "Do I consider myself ugly or ugly looking?" No. I do not consider myself ugly or ugly looking. I consider myself blessed to look the way I do when considering how my face looked in the very beginning. "Do I understand there may be people who consider me ugly looking?" Yes. I understand there will be people who may think of me as ugly looking.

These are the questions that I have asked myself many times. Because of the many surgeries, my face has changed drastically. My surgery results always had me asking and pondering about how I look. In deciding to follow and learn the word of God, another scripture I would be blessed to keep in my thinking is Psalm 139:14 (KJV), "I will praise thee; for I am fearfully [and] wonderfully made: marvellous [are] thy works; and [that] my soul knoweth right well."

I knew how I looked would always be an issue. God had kept me alive. My faith was being strengthened. I learned about beauty from the bible. I recall hearing a woman minister preaching a sermon about Jacob marrying Leah and Rachel. The woman minister said that Leah's eyes were cockeyed. She said Leah was not desirable, she was ugly, and I was floored. I read the many versions of that scripture. I've listed all that I read and compared.

> KJV: Genesis 29:17 "Leah was tender-eyed; but Rachel was beautiful and well-favored."
> NIV: "Leah had weak eyes, but Rachel was lovely in form, and beautiful."
> NLT: "Leah had pretty eyes, but Rachel was beautiful in every way, with a lovely face and shapely figure."
> NASB: "And Leah's eyes were weak, but Rachel was beautiful of form and face. Then there is beautiful Sari, wife of Abram. Abram told Sari you are so beautiful that they will kill me for you, so tell the Egyptians you are my sister not my wife", Genesis 12:11-12. "Let us remember Esther her beauty pleased the king", Esther 2:9.

The bible tells us that the women with beauty played significant roles as everyone does in the bible. However even though the scriptures inform us that Leah was not as beautiful as Rachel, Leah's fourth son Judah would become an ancestor of David and of Jesus Christ because of his son Perez, Ruth 4:18-22, and Matthew 1:3-16. God had a plan for Leah's life. Eventually Leah would be happy. She knew she was fortunate and to be envied because of all her children. Rachel would have Joseph, her only son, but she had Jacobs love.

There are many lessons to learn here. The one that is most important to me is that regardless how you look, God has a purpose and blessings for your life. No matter how I look I intend on building my faith in God who loves me regardless how I look and if no one else loves me, I know that God does. My foundation was strengthened by these women in the bible. I would not be defeated in my life because of how I look. Thank you God, for their lives now help me.

I recall an old black and white movie called "*The Enchanted House*." The story tells of a couple who loved each other so much that they could not see any flaws in their appearance. Everyone else saw them as less than attractive. I learned from this movie that beauty is in the eye of the beholder and beauty is skin deep. I recall as a child a song the Temptations sang called, "*Beauty Is Only Skin Deep*," I liked the song then, I appreciate this song, now. I think this song teaches and encourages those who need it.

My view of the song, "*Beauty Is Only Skin Deep*," is that the man sings about having learned to count on love and that beauty does not mean one will be sincere. I especially like the song expressing words that a person speaks are more meaningful than how a person looks.

I am encouraged by the song that having a pleasing, kind, and loving personality is a rare quality. Going through a traumatic situation can humble you or make you mean. I have been humbled knowing that my personality is a rare quality. I know that beauty is only skin-deep. I also know, depending on the eye of the beholder, it's their judgment. I have learned that some people will judge a person by their wealth, education, beauty, and a prestigious position. My experience has taught me that what looks good can really be harmful.

I have had people who pretended to care about me only because I had something they viewed as important. I have had the experience of having shared my home, money, automobile and knowledge, to find out that people I once associated with wanted what I had and not me.

I have a male family member who had gone through some financial problems. He dated women who could afford him. He told me he only wished he could have what they owned, so he tolerated their presence. Unfortunately, we all play the fool sometimes. Hopefully, we all learn that what is pleasing to the eyes is not always good for your mind.

I have learned that there is beauty in everyone. I understand that societies set standards for beauty. I no longer follow or allow those standards to define what or where I find beauty. I can find beauty in someone's laughter, the tone of their voice, the way they walk, character and/or their personality. I can see beauty in someone's eyes, nose, their hands, arms, hair or no hair. I must admit if the person is evil without regard to others; I can see no beauty. I have learned where there is evil, wrongdoing and unfairness; I can find no beauty.

Though the Waters Run Deep...

Though the waters run deep, I swim,
Though the mountains are high, I climb.
I lift my head to the sky,
I worship God who lives and created on High.
I swim moving always forward towards Him.
~rw 6/7/15

My Faith/Church Life

I needed security and comfort to help me handle how my face looked. I've always been aware that some people can be rude when seeing my face or one who looks physically different. I admit my face has been through many stages of not looking good. In the hospital, I received both security and comfort. I was not exempt in the hospital from folks having remarks or pointing at me. I had hoped because I was in a hospital at least people would know I was seeking help for my face. I can say the insults were few.

I found comfort in bars early in the morning or early afternoon because few people were there. The comfort came from drinking. My reality did strike me while trying to hide behind the wine and music. I quickly left the bar to hide when the truth of my life penetrated the wine and music. I would leave the bar to go home and cry. I made bars my lifestyle for a while. I figured why not, I generally found pity there. My crying led me to a decision to try God with diligence.

I remember the day I was in my bedroom, on the floor, with a bottle of Grand Marnier, Kool cigarettes, and marijuana. I was tired of a life that made no sense and I decided to go to church. I stopped drinking and smoking marijuana because I was paranoid. I thought possibly I would get high and be unable to get sober again. I stopped smoking when the doctor said that it would interfere with the reconstruction of my nose. In an instant, I stopped smoking. I had been a smoker since 14 years of age.

I decided to go to a gym and take care of my body. My thoughts took care of what the fire did not destroy or burn. I knew I was on my way to change. I thought finding a church would be a place of security and comfort. My peace, comfort and rest would be in my relationship with God. I was tired of fighting myself about how I looked. I had exhausted everyone I thought could help me. No one could help me. I knew I needed God. I never realized during those moments of searching that He was guiding me. My spirit knew there was a love like no other that I would encounter. I am so glad that God kept me for Him. I knew I was going somewhere different for the first time in my life. It would not be a person, money or drugs. It would be something that no one could take away from me. My love for my Heavenly Father could not be taken from me. My life was going to mean something. I anticipated great things to happen in my faith and church life.

Often people in church would tell me the Lord said you are going to get a face. I would get sad whenever someone said that to me and many people have. My thought, if you knew what my face looked like before you would know this is my face. My surgeries ended but my face continued to change. I could see physical changes in my facial appearance. My faith had grown and I had changed on the inside. My spirit changed and continues to transition with every new revelation that God shows me. I found that the more I believed for a better face the better my face became to me and others.

I looked for the security and comfort in a church, but the comfort and security would come from me trusting in God. I began to see a pattern form, with me wanting protection from people saying negative things and staring at me. I would quickly learn there was no protection from comments and stares. It would never go away. My challenge would be not to react negatively to comments or stares nor carry a grudge; I learned this quickly, too. I knew that I must not harbor the negative reactions of others. I knew harboring negativity would kill me spiritually. I was physically different and had to find positive ways to deal with hurtful reactions. I asked God for strength and to show me how to live with my physical differences. I received my answer when I read and heard the scripture when Jesus was on the cross. He said, "Forgive them for they know not what they do." (Luke 23:34)

I then realized if people knew how I came to look this way, the pain involved and how I faced death, they would be kind. I am aware there are people who think I was punished or cursed and that's why I was burned. I, too, believed that for a while. I stopped when I understood that preachers get sick and die, people have accidents and life will guarantee some type of horrible pain, whether physical or emotional. I was glad when I was delivered from believing that I had been cursed or was suffering from the sins of my family.

I learned how to handle reactions about how I look. I have been able not to be angry, or sad, about reactions to how I look. I am glad to be alive and to share my love with those who love me regardless of how I look. My standards and Christian lifestyle keep me safe. I have learned to avoid children and teens whether in church or not. It's a heart breaker when youth laugh about how you look. My consistent presence in youthful environments will educate youth and once they know me, it's all good.

I have learned there is a lesson to learn from everyone you meet. I've found it awesome how God uses each of us to teach each of us. I found in church the same rudeness and staring that was in the bars and on the streets. I ran into God in the bar and He showed me my reality. I went to church where Believers go and there God showed me hope, truth, consistency, promises, unconditional love, forgiveness, patience, order, revelations, peace, security, comfort and a transitional me.

I am attentive in church service and anticipate the message that will help make my life better. One of my favorite stories in the bible is about Nebuchadnezzar, a king, Shadrach, Meshach and Abednego.

[Dan 3:14, 15, 24, 26, 28 KJV] 14 "Nebuchadnezzar spake and said unto them, [Is it] true, O Shadrach, Meshach, and Abednego, do not ye serve my gods, nor worship the golden image which I have set up? ... 15 Now if ye be ready that at what time ye hear the sound of the cornet, flute, harp, sackbut, Psalmsltery, and dulcimer, and all kinds of musick, ye fall down and worship the image which I have made; [well]: but if ye worship not, ye shall be cast the same hour into the midst of a burning fiery furnace; and who [is] that God that shall deliver you out of my hands? 16 Shadrach, Meshach, and Abednego, answered and said to the king, O Nebuchadnezzar, we [are] not careful to answer thee in this matter.

17 If it be [so], our God whom we serve is able to deliver us from the burning fiery furnace, and he will deliver [us] out of thine hand, O king. 18 But if not, be it known unto thee, O king, that we will not serve thy gods, nor worship the golden image which thou hast set up. 19 Then was Nebuchadnezzar full of fury, and the form of his visage was changed against Shadrach, Meshach, and Abednego: [therefore] he spake, and commanded that they should heat the furnace one seven times more than it was wont to be heated. 20 And he commanded the most mighty men that [were] in his army to bind Shadrach, Meshach, and Abednego, [and] to cast [them] into the burning fiery furnace. 21 Then these men were bound in their coats, their hosen, and their hats, and their [other] garments, and were cast into the midst of the burning fiery furnace. 22 Therefore because the king's commandment was urgent, and the furnace exceeding hot, the flame of the fire slew those men that took up Shadrach, Meshach, and Abednego.

23 And these three men, Shadrach, Meshach, and Abednego, fell down bound into the midst of the burning fiery furnace. 24 Then Nebuchadnezzar the king was astonied, and rose up in haste, [and] spake, and said unto his counsellors, Did not we cast three men bound into the midst of the fire? They answered and said unto the king, True, O king. ... 26 Then Nebuchadnezzar came near to the mouth of the burning fiery furnace, [and] spake, and said, Shadrach, Meshach, and Abednego, ye servants of the most high God, come forth, and

come [hither]. Then Shadrach, Meshach, and Abednego, came forth of the midst of the fire. ... 28 [Then] Nebuchadnezzar spake, and said, Blessed [be] the God of Shadrach, Meshach, and Abednego, who hath sent his angel, and delivered his servants that trusted in him, and have changed the king's word, and yielded their bodies, that they might not serve nor worship any god, except their own God."

I have heard this story used in many sermons. In anticipation of what is about to be said, I began to feel uncomfortable, because fire is involved. My thoughts are racing with anticipation. I am thinking, "Be careful what you say because fire burned me." I did not walk out of the fire without a scar. My burns were not received because I stood for a cause, or because I stood for God.

I now stand for God and I do have a cause. I started an organization for people with burn injury called *Healed With Scars*. I will speak more about it later. I trust God as those Hebrew men did. Fire causes injury and pain that can cause you to lose your mind. I was delivered from fire, too. I have photos that will show the injury that caused unbelievable pain. I gave birth to a daughter and it was painful. My delivery pain cannot be compared to the pain I have endured from skin grafts and wound changes, with medication. I know the pain of fire was so horrible on my face that I passed out. I cannot remember the pain of the actual burning. I do know the pain of the injury.

God delivered the Hebrew men and God delivered me. I know the Hebrew men came out without any signs of injury from fire and they went into the fire knowing God. I came out of a fiery furnace knowing God. When I had the accident, my relationship with God consisted of thoughts of a God. I know that when the Hebrew men came out of the fire their faith in God was made stronger. My injuries are scars now that remind me how God has delivered me. My faith has been made strong because of my experience with fire. I know I am alive and I know only a loving God, my Father in Heaven, has made me whole.

I am thankful for churches and organizations who Believe God. I have learned to grow into a better person when I am surrounded by people who have transitioned into being their best selves according to God's ways.

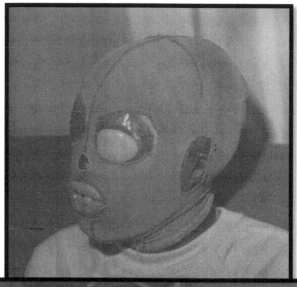

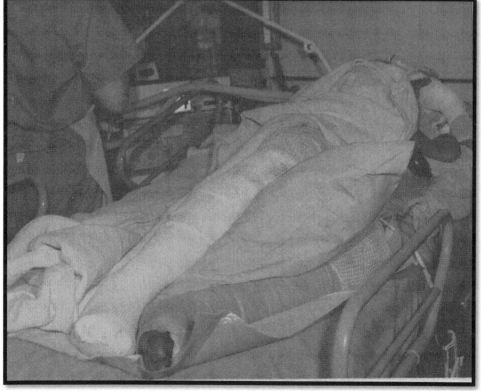

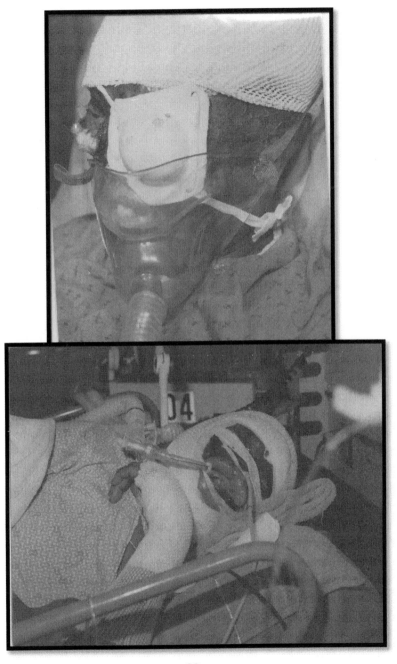

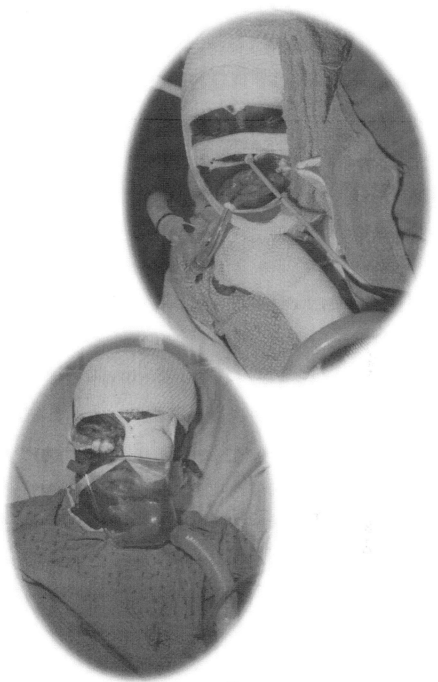

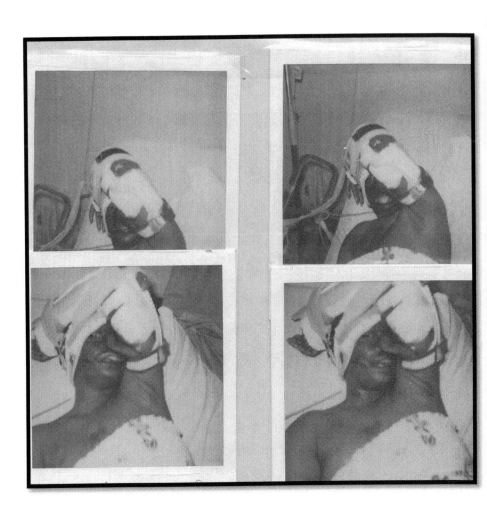

What I Didn't Know

I didn't know that people would laugh at me because of how I looked.

I didn't know if I shared my story, that I still wouldn't receive understanding about the pain I suffered.

I didn't know that I would be called names referencing my injuries.

I didn't know that I would be laughed at about the result of my injuries.

I didn't know that I would be taken advantage of because of how I look.

I didn't know for a while that I would love others more than myself.

I didn't know that I would be abandoned because of how I look.

I didn't know that I would not be loved because of how I look.

I didn't know that my love would be taken for granted.

I didn't know that I would constantly be proving myself worthy.

I didn't know that when I started living for God I
would still be rejected.

I didn't know that my chances for discrimination
would magnify for rejection because of facial burns
because:
A. I am a woman in a man's world
B. I am a Black woman
C. I am not a wealthy woman
D. I am, according to society, not an attractive
woman
E. I do not have a PhD
F. I am a Christian

I didn't know when I worked hard to be a woman of
God that I would be hated.

I didn't know that seeking God diligently would
protect me.

I didn't know that my praise for God would be
mocked.

I didn't know I would be called crazy because of how
I look.

I didn't know it would take prayer for me to have
courage to go outside.

I didn't know I could walk away from sin until I
served God.

I didn't know God was waiting for me.

When It Gets Hard

I have learned that when you have overcome many things, such as being blind in one eye and learning to drive with one eye, that is overcoming. I will talk about my blindness throughout because there are more things to share with you. I now find it's not a big deal to drive with one eye, but when I couldn't manage driving as I did with two eyes, it was a big deal. I've been driving with one eye about 20 years. I learned how to walk using a walker and therapy. I had to overcome many physical issues. My overcoming is a large part of my life today with the help of God and other people. My overcoming is consistent, life and living is about a constant moving. I find even when I think my life has settled, it's still moving. That's God, moving things for His purpose.

When problems of life become difficult, I expect not to fail because I have been through many ordeals. I find if things don't go the way I want, I am always blessed with a lesson. These ordeals have caused me to cry and suffer through the pain that connects with it. I will be sharing throughout the book about my physical and mental pain. I have had pain so horrible I thought I would die. I was given Morphine to ease those types of pains. I have experienced the pain of wound cleaning. Burn wounds that have no skin covering, pink flesh exposed that has been covered with bandages, now have to be cleaned and re-bandaged.

When relationships and financial problems happen, there is no nurse giving me Morphine. I have been trained in pain and "trauma." My training has been receiving over a hundred surgeries. I have found surgeries to be lifesaving, and a healthy way to rid illness. My experiences in surgery are submitting myself, my life, to practicing doctors. My choices for facial reconstruction were with limits. I faced every surgery not knowing the outcome, but expecting a great outcome. I found that traumatic.

I find that hurt and worry does not last when I seek God and face my concerns right away. My challenge is thinking that I can handle the problem without seeking God. I am learning to seek God at the onset of anything that could possibly be a potential problem. I do not like mess in my life so I seek God for direction. I follow God's direction easily when I am in trauma mode. My trauma mode is there if there is no answer that humanly works. I shift quickly from worry to trusting in God to following His direction. I am glad that God tells us how to think. I am glad for my relationship with God. When I had my accident, my relationship with God was the beginning of a new way to live, to be. Philippians 4:8 "Finally, brethren, whatsoever things are true, whatsoever things [are] honest, whatsoever things [are] just, whatsoever things [are] pure, whatsoever things [are] lovely, whatsoever things [are] of good report; if [there be] any virtue, and if [there be] any praise, think on these things."

I have learned in hard times to draw close to God. I do and think everything spiritual. This is my defense. I am in wartime mode. My bible reading, praying and fasting increases. I make it a point to speak to spirit minded people for encouragement and direction. I avoid anything or anyone who can shift my faith to doubt. Being a blessing and praying for those who are going through hard times is part of my defense. My memories of past hard times such as death and illness are a reminder that the hard times will pass. I can look back and see what I did or what I didn't do. I made writing in a journal part of my defense. I find reading about coming through a bad situation is better than recalling. My journal is evidence I survived the hard time.

I know preparation for tough times is important. When surprised by a hard time, I pray immediately and won't get up until God says so. I learned that every traumatic situation is different. My financial resources and the people who played important roles during the last hard time may have changed. I found it important to know whom you can depend upon for certain things. My scheduled surgeries gave me time to prepare. I can choose who can take me to hospital, pick me up from hospital and speak to my doctor if I am unable to.

I find that when life gets hard, facing that real hard thing first clears my head to think. I now say, how will this hard thing be resolved and proceed to find the way that leads to overcoming. I know through experience waiting for someone to do it for me is not the answer. I know that no one wants your hard times and few people want to be near. I find that it is not a bad thing. I only want folks around who been through a hard time and understand the pain I am experiencing.

I had an aunt who lived to 82 years of age. I saw in her life that the hard times were there until her death. I watched how she dealt with her hard times. I saw her do what she could and she kept on smiling as if there were no hard times. I watched my mother continue through her hard times and I listened to her say, "When my job shut down, my life changed." I have been given advice about hard times and I have given advice. My take-away from the seniors in my family is to prepare by asking God for direction, seeking direction, use the directions for your hard times, fear not and trust God.

The Real Deal

I recall throughout my youth the inspiration and hope I would receive from the adults in my family and their friends. I was complimented as being pretty, smart and could sing. I was never told I could dance. I am laughing, I managed to get by. Conversations I would hear from adult family members would be, "Oh yeah, Rose is going to be somebody." I remember my daddy taking me to Speakeasy's on Fridays and Saturdays. A Speakeasy is a place where liquor and beer is sold. Daddy did not take me regularly, but often. I was told to sing at the Speakeasy. Daddy would say, "Rose get up there and sing." I would sing and get a quarter. I remember one of my favorite songs to sing was by Stevie Wonder, *The Answer My Friend is Blowing in the Wind.* I loved that song.

I was strongly encouraged in my elementary school, Alexander Wilson School. I believed our teachers. They said if we listened and did what we were being taught, we would go far and do great things in our lives. We were taught respect, honor, discipline and to work hard. My encouragement would come from church and a recreational facility with adults who inspired me. I attended a church called "Paradise Baptist Church", Reverend Daniel Williamson was the Pastor. Reverend Williamson came to my bedside in the hospital to pray for me when I had my accident.

I remember Reverend Williamson saying, "Rose, pray for yourself," and I did. I promised Reverend Williamson that I would preach one day. I was in a highly spiritual state of mind. I sang on the choir at Paradise Baptist Church, read the weekly announcements, attended Sunday school regularly and was called a church girl by the boys in the neighborhood.

The recreational center, Johnson Playground, was directly across the street from my home. I ran track and competed, played checkers well enough to compete and played ping-pong well. My participation in these places and activities gave me confidence. I believed that I would be unique in my life and successful as defined during those years. During those years, success meant obtaining a job, graduating high school, getting married and having a house. I believed that I would obtain this success in my early teens.

I remember a movie titled *"Splendour in the Grass."* The movie starred Natalie Wood and Warren Beatty. I have viewed this movie in my youth, teen and adult years. I had different thoughts each time I saw the movie. The movie tells of two young lovers and how they were separated by choices they made. The movie goes into their adulthood showing the journey of both people. The journey shows their pain, their hope, their differences and most of all, their love. A love that was lost.

I have repeatedly been enlightened by the poem used in the movie. The poem was written by William Wordsworth (April 7, 1770 – April 23, 1850). William Wordsworth was a romantic poet and his sister, Dorothy Wordsworth was a poet, both from England. The siblings were a year apart in age and they were very close. Their father John Wordsworth separated William and Dorothy when their mother died. William was sent to Bangor Grammar School and Dorothy was sent to live with relatives in Yorkshire. William and Dorothy would see each other nine years later.

I read this poem and I remember in my youth, hope radiated my being. My facial injuries caused me to lose confidence in my future. I agreed with the poem when it states, "Though nothing can bring back the hour of splendor in the grass, of glory in the flower." My dreams of being a good-looking woman, receiving love from a man, having a job, being accepted, were gone. I would only have memories of the hour when my life was splendor. I read the poem and realized that I must not grieve but find the strength that I had acquired and take it with me as I transition.

I knew the sympathy and pain that I initially felt would be a memorable point in my life, it will always be. My thoughts of my suffering did soon calm me, for the suffering was over. My faith endured the shadow of death and the years of this experience will bring me to a philosophic mind. I never would have guessed or thought that the many times I saw the movie *Splendour in the Grass,* that the poem would have such meaning in my life.

My dreams, hopes and confidence changed when my face was burned. I processed many thoughts on overcoming and becoming somebody of substance. My pain was indescribable, unspeakable. I knew of no one who had suffered what I was suffering. I knew there had to be someone who had suffered the physical and emotional pain. I met an Italian guy in the St. Agnes Hospital named Nino Nardy who was burned. Nino was kind to me and shared his experience. I lost contact with him and was saddened. My conclusion to all of the pain and confronting my face, was nothing could bring back the hour of splendor in the grass.

I read a book titled "*Autobiography of a Face*" by Lucy Grealy. My emotions were elevated. I experienced through Lucy's writings what it was like as a child with cancer in her face and not being able to have surgeries until her teens and adulthood. I cried for a child who had to experience the things I had experienced as an adult. I cried about the physical pain she endured through her chemotherapy treatments.

I understood her feelings of ugliness, hiding her face, trying to understand other's feelings about her illness, being teased by boys in school, and wondering if she would ever be loved by a man. I was saddened that she died at the age of thirty-nine. Lucy was born in Ireland in 1963 died in 2002. I was helped knowing that I, too, have had and still can feel the way Lucy felt because of how her face looked. I agree with Lucy. A face disfigured will limit you in relationships and especially those of love. I was reminded of the painful experiences of having a disfigured face while hoping surgery will make my face acceptable.

I spent many years watching television because of surgeries, recovery, finances, and because going outside with how I looked took great preparation mentally and emotionally. I watched many talk shows during my years of being indoors.

I watched Oprah and read Susan Taylor's column in the "*Essence*" magazine. People have said great and bad things about Oprah. I give her praise and honor. I watched Oprah speak on many topics. Oprah gave me hope and told her viewers there was hope. I am thankful for the effort and pain that she went through to keep a television show such as hers broadcasting. I am thankful for Susan Taylor for the advice and hope she wrote in "*Essence*" magazine.

I am overjoyed with the many women who speak on topics to help women overcome heartache, abuse, illnesses, and financial issues. I am a witness to the cruelty that men are able to do to women. I know that a man can encourage or destroy a woman with his words, like no woman can. I am glad for the men who stand up for justice for women. I understand the time women live in today, but it is still a man's world. I recall James Brown singing a man's world would be nothing without a woman or a girl.

A woman or a girl can be destroyed by a man's words. I have found the word of God is stronger than any man's word and God's word will heal what a man's word almost killed. I thank you, Lucy Grealy, for sharing your story about the men in your life.

I know the reality of my life had to be faced just as Lucy's. I know the real deal can be painful from people I love.

My family and friends appeared to have lost hope. I do know the few family and friends who thought I would make it through. I am aware that everybody agreed and knew except me in the beginning, that my face was gone forever. My face would only be remembered in photos and the resemblances of relatives. I heard many conversations of defeat related to my overcoming the physical and emotional trials. I know many people said I wouldn't make it. I heard a song on the radio one day sitting in my bedroom while I lived at my grandmother's house.

The song is titled, *"I'm Still Holding On,"* written by Luther Barnes and sung by Deborah Barnes. I cried the first time I heard this song. I was inspired to fight for my life every time I heard it. My moments of fear and discouragement fade away when I hear this song. I am reminded of how far the Lord has brought me.

I think of how many people expressed with their conversations that I wouldn't have a future, but this day proves that I am still holding on and moving forward in my life. I had many supporters who said they would be with me. My supporters, my friends and some family left.

My transitions in my recovery process of healing gave me cause to end relationships. I was intent on healing and living a great life. I saw people who were dear to me were not seeing my vision for my life. At fourteen, I remember walking down the street on the block where I lived. I knew there was something about God and me. I said to God, "Why am I feeling alone walking down this hilly pavement hill? I sense I will be alone when I grow up." I had no response from God.

I only thought of my words to God when I found myself feeling lonely. I said to God during that walk, "Wherever I am, just don't leave me, but show me the way." The words of the song, *"I'm Still Holding On,"* say the road has been rough and the going has been tough but I am not leaving God.

My thirty years of living without my born face has been rough, I have been laughed at, pointed at, I've been criticized for believing that if I live like God says, I'll be alright. I know for certain without God, my life was in turmoil on a regular basis and that's why I know I am still in His Holy plan. I know many will still scandalize my name but I am going to Hold ON like the song sings.

My conversation with God was like this, "I know you are with me, God, because no one can help me but You." I know this is and has been "The Real Deal."

Feelings

My feelings in the beginning of my many faces:

I read these verses in Psalms 38 and knew from verses 11 – 21, these were my feelings.

Psalms 38:11   My friends and companions avoid me because of my wounds; my neighbors stay far away.

Psalms 38:12 Those who want to kill me set their traps, those who would harm me talk of my ruin; all day long they scheme and lie.

Psalms 38:13 I am like the deaf, who cannot hear, like the mute, who cannot speak;

Psalms 38:14 I have become like one who does not hear, whose mouth can offer no reply.

Psalms 38:15 LORD, I wait for you; you will answer, Lord my God.

Psalms 38:16 For I said, "Do not let them gloat or exalt themselves over me when my feet slip."

Psalms 38:17 For I am about to fall, and my pain is ever with me.

Psalms 38:18 I confess my iniquity; I am troubled by my sin.

Psalms 38:19 Many have become my enemies without cause; those who hate me without reason are numerous.

Psalms 38:20 Those who repay my good with evil lodge accusations against me, though I seek only to do what is good.

Psalms 38:21 LORD, do not forsake me; do not be far from me, my God.

1. I wanted my family and friends to know what I was living with. I wanted them to know my pain, my fear and my life.
2. I just want to be happy.
3. My scars, will they go away?
4. I really do look like a monster from television; help me to get out of this body. I cry.
5. My nose, my eyes, my mouth are not the same, help me somebody, no help me God. I cry.
6. I will never wear earrings again.
7. My daughter, will she be afraid of me with this messed up face?
8. My daughter, will she still love me?
9. No eyelids, no nose!
10. My whole body scarred for life, I cry.
11. I pose for a photographer, a white man, to take naked pictures of me at my mother's house. I stand with arms stretched out wide, he says look this way, now turn around so he can take photos from behind, I am naked. I cry on the inside, no tears. I am numb. The photos were for my legal case. My mind is lost.

12. My family and friends say I will never be anything, they mean no future, but they say, "never be anything." I cry to myself, God please help me, I am hopeless.

13. Forgive me, God, I have sinned. I am being punished.

14. No one comes to see me; no one calls.

15. I look at the chipped painted green walls and I cry.

16. I am living dead!

17. I am in the beginning of my suffering, God help me, I am scared.

18. Why do you look at me, while you hold back your laughter?

19. I am ugly; are my thoughts?

20. My family, I am in my thirties. Why do you speak and treat me like I am retarded? (mentally challenged was not used then)

21. My family, why do you treat me like a toddler?

22. I sit in my hospital bed and point to my daughter's photo; she is seven.

23. I can't walk; I have one eye, help me.

24. I wanted my family to know when I went to the doctor for my face; it was a big deal.

25. I wanted my family to know that my life was crazy, not normal. Who has to have a face rebuilt, oh, me!

26. I was certain that my ex-husband would never leave me, how could he? I had no face, one eye, and surgeries for the next year, so I thought.

27. I go to therapy for a dressing change for my buttocks, I cry, I scream the pain when the therapist removed the dressing and cleaned the wound. The morphine was not enough to stop the pain.

28. My veins in my arms, my wrist and my hand are no longer good for giving blood. The doctor says take it from her neck, I plead and cry please I am afraid. They take blood from my leg.

29. I will always have to hide. My nose will never look normal. Ugly people call me ugly. I am pretty. I had an accident. I was not born this way. People don't care.

30. I am in church, a sister, a Christian friend, asked me about my breathing, but she is mocking me, she pretends to care. I see you watch me and laugh. You hurt me. I am sad.

31. My daughter, I cannot walk her to school. I don't want other children to know I am her mother, because I know my face looks scary to children.

32. My husband could never bear to kiss or hold me ever again. Who have I become?

33. The photo of me in the hospital with tubes in my mouth and nostril; my skin looks like a burnt hot dog.

34. I must be strong, I must hold on because I don't want to lose my mind.

35. Does anyone know what I am going through?

36. I don't want to go outside on Halloween. A man said you have a nice costume. I cry inside, I say to myself, "The costume is real."

37. I cannot run from myself.

38. I want to be pretty again.

39. I want my daddy. I want my father. No one sees me anymore.

40. I had to believe that something would happen, to make things change.

41. I have to love myself.

42. I struggled, I cried, I prayed, I feared, but I could not hate.

43. I wanted to be angry but I could not.

44. Family and friends, your feelings matter to me. I am sorry that my burnt face and body have affected your life.

45. I don't know where to run. I want to hide from my family, but my daughter wants me.

46. I must hold on; find a way to stay sane so no one takes my daughter.

47. God, here am I. Show me the way and I will follow.

48. All I can do is trust and wait as I navigate a new life, a new world of rejection.

The Men (the Samsons in my life) Who Taught Me

I read the biblical story of Samson and Delilah. Samson's story is found in Judges, chapters 13-16. An angel of the Lord told Samson's parents that their son would help begin to set Israel free from the Philistines. The Spirit of the Lord was with Samson; he had great strength. Samson fell in love with Delilah. The Philistines hired Delilah to find out how Samson acquired his physical strength.

Delilah consistently tried to find out where Samson's strength came from. Samson would soon tell Delilah about his hair and his relationship with God from birth. I love a love story with a happy ending; however, the only person in love was Samson. I was always critical about Samson not seeing the game being played on him and the evil being formed against him, until it happened to me.

I have heard men and women of God say to single Christians, "Beware of people who are unequally yoked with you and seek you for a relationship." I recall my Bishop saying that people are fine in saying no to people who don't appeal to you. However, when the person you are attracted to comes along and you know you are unequally yoked, the possibility of denying the person can be unlikely.

I never thought after my accident that I would not be able to have male relationships and the possibility of marriage again. My life long pretty looks were gone and new looks would come yearly following surgeries. I never saw myself as ugly or unattractive. My ex-husband said that I was an ugly, burnt, black, snot nosed, (the bad word) female dog. My ex-husband said no one would want me.

I have experienced those times when men have rudely responded to me. I would walk to the stores in Philly where men in cars would see my face and say some things that I thought would physically kill me on the spot because I allowed it to penetrate my spirit and soul.

In spite of my facial injuries, there would be male relationships before accepting Christ and after accepting Christ into my life. In my thirty years of being a woman with facial injury, I learned from the brothers/men who entered my life. I will call them all Samson except my ex-husband. I will number them in the order each came into my life. I will name the first one Samson #1BC. Before Christ is BC or Samson#1AC, After Christ.

I decided to call all of them Samson because I believe God uses all of us. Samson in the bible had great potential. Samson's story in Judges tells how he was born and how he started his life with credentials, with promise. His mother, during her pregnancy, had a special diet prohibiting her from eating anything off a vine and any unclean thing. I have learned that we may all have potential, but it means nothing if we use it wrong or don't use it at all.

I think it's awesome to be separated from the world and consecrated to God. I, being a Believer of the Lord, know it can be hard. Fred Hammond sings in the song titled *Order My Steps* and says, "When you are called by God sometimes it just don't feel good, it's just down right uncomfortable." I have found in my walk of faith in the challenging times, I wanted to do it my way and not God's way.

I have to ask myself, "Did you learn the lesson or have you forgotten when you avoid God's way, you run into natural and spiritual trouble?" I have found, as with Samson, during the times of relationships when love and lust is involved, it can be hard when the Holy Spirit and the ways of God say, "No, you cannot love that person."

I've mentioned the recreation center called Johnsons now named 48th & Woodland Avenue Recreation Center across the street from my childhood home. I met my ex-husband in that playground. He was playing basketball with a few other guys from a street gang called Woodland Avenue. I and other young teens ranging from 14 – 18 were sitting on the benches near the basketball court.

We were laughing and playing around. Suddenly my ex-husband had a knife enter his thigh. All the teens ran over to see. I asked, "Do you want to go to the hospital?" He said, "I want you to go with me." Wow, I can still smile about his response. Rose, the teen, just showed up.

My ex was taken to Mercy Douglas Hospital. I went to the hospital with a few of my girlfriends. I remember seeing his mother there, how beautiful I thought she was. My ex and I exchanged phone numbers and a relationship started. We were married in our home, a duplex he purchased. Our wedding was small; a few of our closest family members. Reverend Daniel Williamson married us, the same reverend who told me to pray for myself when he visited me in the burn unit.

My father walked with me and gave me to Mr. Washington to marry. Mr. & Mrs. Washington were married June 5, 1976 and Nneka Sharifa Washington was born March 15, 1978. On June 19, 1992, Mr. & Mrs. Washington were divorced. Our daughter is married and birthed two children who are loved by both grandparents.

I have wondered and pondered over the end of my marriage. My marriage was not healthy when I experienced my near fatal accident. My coming home from the hospital would end up being sad for me. My reality was my marriage was fading into no marriage. My husband would never kiss me, hold or love me again.

My husband said I was cursed. I believed him at times. I said to myself, "Look at what has happened to me. I am blind, I am helpless and I have no hope." I had come home but I was alienated from all the people I knew.

I recall having to go to family court for child support. I wore my facial mask (called job) with an egg-shaped plastic that covered the flesh of where my eye once was. My ex did not want to pay child support. My ex argued with the staff. The courts granted me money that was needed for me and our daughter, who was seven.

I tried to live with my ex after coming home but he possessed a hatred that I could not understand. In our home, he avoided me as if I had a plague. I stayed about a week with him and then returned to my mother's home where I initially stayed once leaving the hospital.

I stayed with my mother for a while and she, too, had a problem with me living there. My mother said it was hard to look at me and it was easier for her if I lived with my grandmother. My daughter and I moved in with my grandmother into her front bedroom.

Samson#1BC

I began talking on the phone to Samson#1BC. Samson#1BC was incarcerated and would be for twenty-five years. I looked at those years as being a lifetime. I, too, was incarcerated in a body that I wanted to be freed from. Samson#1BC had beaten someone to near death. My thinking, at the time, was I did not know the truth and did not try to find out. I wanted someone to talk to me. Samson#1BC had no idea what I looked like even though I told him.

My mother knew about the phone calls and objected. Once she heard and saw me on the phone with Samson#1BC and snatched the phone from my hand and hung it up. My mother said, "Do you realize the phone bill you will have to pay?" My mother was right. My mother asked me what did I think could come of me talking to Samson#1BC. I knew nothing and I told her nothing.

I had not thought of the telephone charges. I thought of my loneliness. I thought of how my mother avoided me with the exception of bringing me food and seeing if my daughter was all right. My mother never came to visit, to sit and talk. I began reading the bible while Samson#1BC was still in my life.

I found myself paying large phone bills and I knew I could not afford the calls. I cut the calls down and began to write letters to Samson#1BC. My husband, like my mother, avoided me. I noticed after my ex stopped speaking to me; my conversations with Samson#1BC changed. The conversations became sexual. I know now that if my family had not shut me out, but talked to me, there would not have been Samson#1BC. I was desperate for love and attention. I needed to know I still belonged to my family.

My family members watched me as if I were an animal in the zoo. I felt I looked like one, too. I knew I had to turn to God for help. I was scared. I was being avoided by the most important people in my life, except when there was need or business to be handled. I was about to hit panic mode. I began reading the bible. I started with Samson#1BC who was still in my life. I took note that Samson#1BC could not help me financially, spiritually or with my family reactions to me. He appealed to my flesh. Samson#1BC reminded me I was a woman.

I would speak with family members of Samson#1BC. I believed that speaking with his family validated my emotional feelings for Samson#1BC. I believed we had a lot in common. I went to visit Samson#1BC and the reality of how I looked struck me cold. I wore the job mask, a tight fitting garment all over my body. I wore the plastic egg shape covering for the eye that had been burned away.

I traveled by plane to see Samson#1BC. Samson#1BC appeared to be intoxicated, and he was. I thought, "How does one get high in jail?" Samson#1BC said he never had a visitor from home to come see him. I felt ashamed and rejected. He couldn't look at me. I remembered no part of the conversation.

I went home trying to convince myself everything went well. My mother was pissed when she figured out I went to visit Samon#1BC in prison. I had hoped my ex-husband never found out. I would end the relationship after nine months when Samson#1BC asked me to participate in illegal schemes and buy him clothing.

I believed at the time I had a lot in common with Samson#1BC but there were many things that were not common. The common thing was the isolation our situations placed us in. I knew a few issues were affecting both Samson#1BC and I. I knew there would be no immediate help or change in our situations. A negative reputation would be attached to both of us for a long time. Samson#1BC's negative reputation would come from his reason for being locked up. My negative reputation would be nothing good can come from a face destroyed by fire.

My differences from Samson#1BC are I committed no crime, I was not sentenced to years of imprisonment, I had the freedom to move about, I was near family and friends where opportunity for change could happen, I could meet new people at the hospital and my daughter was with me.

My common things with Samson#1BC were things that appeared to be permanent. I learned that tragedy can fool a person into believing there is no hope. I heard that Samson#1BC did his time and came home; even his sentence was not permanent. I learned, guilty or not, endurance is a must if one desires to come out of a tragic situation. My experience has shown me that love from family and friends is the best medicine when going through a traumatic situation. Love, patience, compassion and the desire to help is necessary. It helps if there are many people who are willing to give love and compassion. Caregivers need to be cared for also.

Samson#2BC

My life continued to be full of surgeries and doctor visits. My looks were changing slowly. I have a childhood friend who I've known since she was five years old. I love her dearly. My childhood friend had a boyfriend who was in jail who introduced me to Samson#2BC. I thought that brothers in jail would be good for talking on the phone. I wasn't going to any places. My life was filled with my young daughter who had not reached preteen age. My life was filled with recuperating and resting. I did not have to pay phone bills for Samson#2BC.

I believed that conversing with brothers in jail was a substitute replacement for my loneliness I was experiencing. My loneliness was the result of my ex-husband distancing himself from me. I remember when my father went to jail for owing tickets; that's what I was told. My dad did three months for unpaid tickets.

I remember when my dad came home, family and friends were happy. My daddy was tall and good-looking. His complexion and smile with his gold tooth radiated. My mother said the gold tooth was a country thing, a style.

My daddy walked me to school wearing an unbuttoned black trench coat and it moved with his stride. My dad walked with his stroll and he looked regal. I knew there would probably be an argument with Mommy and Daddy about him finding work. I knew that Daddy would probably go to the bars on Woodland Avenue to see his friends. I hoped he didn't come home drunk, but I was glad he was home. I remember in my youth fathers, brothers and uncles were always going to jail for something.

Samson#2BC had been put in jail for some illegal activities. I visited him in the Holmesburg Prison in Philadelphia a few times before he was sent to Dallas, a prison in Pennsylvania. I remember Samson#2BC had to go to court and he wanted me to come and be a character witness. I agreed. I went to City Hall and actually was sworn in and said how kind he had been in spite of how I looked. My friend Samson#2BC was sentenced to seven years.

My relationship with Samson#2BC lasted several months. I ended the relationship after he asked me to help organize transportation of rims with some friends he had on the outside. I became fearful and broke all ties with him. I had met his mother and sister at his trial they were nice people. I stayed in contact with his family for a while. I really liked Samson#2BC. He knew all the right things to say to make me feel like a young, good-looking woman. I needed a fantasy because my reality was hell.

I saw Samson#2BC after he did his seven years. I met him at his mother's house. I had changed drastically with my looks, thinking and finances. Samson#2BC said that my face looked good. The last time Samson#2BC saw me I wore a veil similar to what the Muslim sisters wear. Samson#2BC liked that because he was Muslim.

My phone relationships with Samson#1BC and #2BC kept discussions about my facial burns and surgeries to a minimum. I liked it that way. I always felt like I was without facial injury when we spoke.

I drove a 1998 560SEC Mercedes, black with burgundy interior. I remember when Samson#2BC would talk about the cars we wanted to drive. I was glad to share with him what I was driving. He liked my car. Samson#2BC wanted me to accommodate a physical need. I said no. My thought was he had been incarcerated for seven years and the possibility he could have been with a man stuck in my mind. I also knew that AIDS was running rampant during this time.

My life was just starting to come together. I knew it would be the last time I saw him, because I had no intention of risking my safety or my money. My conversation with him signaled he still thought criminally minded. Years later, I would see him driving a car with an older woman who he introduced as his wife. I smiled, greeted his wife and congratulated him.

I promised myself never would I talk to incarcerated men. I had started talking to Samson#2BC while living at my grandmother's house. I had grown bored with the fantasies incarcerated men provided. I knew if they were home, I would not be their first choice. I knew it was time for a change to handle my loneliness.

Samson#2BC said to me he was having a conversation with a lifer in prison. The lifer said to him at least you only have seven years and you will be free. Samson#2BC said that the lifer must be crazy if he thinks that seven years is ok to be in prison. I understand that from the lifer's perspective, Samson#2BC had hope. I understand from Samson#2BC that seven years at the start of his imprisonment seemed hopeless. I learned that whatever your situation is, someone can have it worse and never give up hope.

I received a Social Security check for $2,500. This was money owed because they overlooked my daughter when calculating my Social Security benefits. I told my mother about the money and said it would be good if we, my daughter and I, could live with her. I asked if she would look for a house big enough. My brother and sister still lived with my mother. My mother said she would and she found a large home with enough room for all of us.

I had been living with my grandmother for a while and I was getting tired of the lifestyle. My uncle, my mom's brother and grandmother's son is mentally challenged, but he drank alcohol and so did my grandmother. I had to watch both of them as if they were toddlers. I would set soda cans on the stair steps so I could hear him coming or going late at night when my grandmother and I were asleep. My uncle would bring women who used crack into the house (aka crack heads). I knew they were trying to steal and he was having lust attacks.

Samson#3BC

I had packed and we were moving. I gave mommy all the money to use for the move. My daughter and I had the largest bedroom. My sister had the middle bedroom, mommy had the back bedroom and my brother had the entire cellar. We were happy. I met Samson#3BC from someone who knew Samson#2BC. I thought, at least Samson#3BC was not incarcerated. I would find that Samson#3BC was imprisoned with crack. I, too, would become crack addicted.

I was addicted for three months. My social security check would come and I would call Samson#3BC. My part for the rent, bills and food were given to my mother. Any money left went up in crack smoke. I thought it was good until there was no more. I had been talking with my lawyers and they were scheduling me for my deposition. I was certain the case money was coming soon. I thought to myself what if I got high off crack and never got sober again. I knew I would be receiving a lot of money, I thought to myself, "I could kill myself smoking this stuff." I was scared of crack.

I got on my knees and cried out to God in Heaven and said, "I am going to die if you don't help me." I begged God. My God answered my prayer. I was no longer hooked. I was thankful; unbelievable, it was a miracle. I soon stopped seeing Samson#3BC because he could no longer smoke crack with me or near me. I received a phone call months later after I stopped seeing Samson#3BC. It was from his mother. I couldn't understand what she was saying. Samson#3BC's mother said, "He is gone." I said, "Who is gone, and gone where?" She said he was dead.

I went to her house soon after she said this. Samson#3BC had been stabbed to death. Samson#3BC was not a thug. Samson#1 & 2 were thugs. My heart was broken. I went to his funeral and I couldn't believe it was him. I had to say goodbye when he was living because his crack habit could have killed me. I believe his crack habit got him killed.

I moved out the large house my mother found for all of us to live together. I liked my new home. I had a friend who was helpful in helping me move. I gave her money and she got people from the neighborhood to clean and paint the house. I was able to mourn in my own home away from my mother and siblings. I was hurt and crying about Samson#3BC.

I believed he loved me. Samson#3BC never mentioned how I looked. He always complimented me when I got dressed; he said I looked nice. He was 8 years younger than I. I was 35. Samson#3BC was tall, dark skinned and slender. I liked his shape; it was similar to my ex-husband. I always liked slow dancing with my ex-husband and two-stepping (aka stranding). I would ask Samson#3BC to two-step with me; he never knew it reminded me of dancing with my ex-husband.

I was sad and angry that Samson#3BC could not stop using crack. I learned that I might have had a scarred face, but I believed that there was more for me in my life. I could not understand the lives of Samson's#1, 2, & 3BC, their lives filled with lies and confusion. I was growing.

I had moments I really thought my husband was fleeing from me with no intent of returning. My thoughts came true. My ex-husband and I have known each other since he was 16 and I, 14. To flee from me at a traumatic time was unbearable. I experienced moments where I hurt so badly because he didn't call or visit. I felt like my life had ended. My burns seemed easy in comparison to my ex-husband not being present in my life or our daughter's life.

I received one hundred thousand dollars from the church who owned the van that hit my car sending it into a tree exploding with me in it and being thrown from the car on fire. I received the check in both my husband and my name. My ex-husband came and we went to cash it. I do not recall giving him any money. I do know he would be receiving money from the lawsuit regarding my injuries.

I can still see him smiling as he left me. I wondered why he was leaving. I loved the song that we once called our song by Al Green, "*Let's Stay Together.*" I thought, "Have you forgotten the words?" I thought, especially the lyrics "whether times are good or bad happy or sad."

My days were looking prosperous and I was feeling good. I was still having surgeries. My ex-husband did not know about them. I bought a GMC, Jimmy Jeep, black on black. I liked it because it had my daddy's name. I paid my grandmother money I owed her and paid off my daughter's tuition at St. Francis De Sales School. I bought my mom a little car. I was being watched by Samson#4BC. Samson#4BC worked in the area near to my home.

Samson#4BC

I could not believe that Samson#4BC was interested in me. I found him funny, cute, and he had brown eyes. I had fun with him for six months and then the fantasy stopped. I phoned his home and a lady answered. I asked to speak with him and she said this is Mrs. Samson#4BC. I said, "Hello, may I speak with your son?" Mrs. Samson#4BC said, "No, fool, I am his wife." I hung up the phone.

I immediately received a call from Samson#4BC. His explanation was it was his sister playing a joke. I hear a voice say, "I am on the line (his wife). Tell her you're married or get out." I hang up. My thought was a half a glass of water was better than none. I had already determined in my mind if he came around, I would let him in. I cried that night believing that I would always be the other woman because of how I looked.

I recall Samson#4BC saying the sweetest things to me all the time. I soon learned that snorting cocaine was his addiction. Samson#4BC would say things like, "People don't understand that I love you." Samson#4BC was there when I received two million dollars. He never knew how much I had but he would soon learn it was a lot.

I purchased him clothing so he would look stylish. I bought him jewelry. All I bought for him had to stay at my home. I was enjoying the glamourous life with Samson#4BC. I took him on trips and we stayed in first class hotels. Samson#4BC purchased his cocaine; I bought the alcohol.

I had a bar in my Lansdowne home with an in-ground pool with a heater, fireplace, electric garage, lower level solarium, Jacuzzi, a marble shower and bathroom, surround-sound on the deck and throughout the house. I had a Mercedes Benz and a jeep. My home was furnished with quality furniture. My daughter and I had cell phones before they became popular. The phones looked like walkie-talkies.

My patience was growing thin with Samson#4BC when I began to notice a pattern. Samson#4BC had four children that I knew of. Samson#4BC would stay regularly with me for a while and then go with his baby mommas usually two to three months at a time.

I remember Samson#4BC said to me, "I am going to lie to you and you are going to like it." My face was struck with a dumb look. Samson#4BC was already lying to me and I thought it was evident I liked it because I continued with the relationship.

My cousin in Wilmington, Delaware invited me to visit. I took Samson#4BC with me. My cousin said, "You are getting rid of him." My cousin said, "Do you remember who you are?" My cousin and I are the same age and first cousins. My dad and my cousin's mother were sister and brother. My cousin and I were called the pretty and smart girls in the family.

I told my cousin I didn't know how to let him leave, that I loved him. My cousin said, "No, you don't love him." I told her she was right. My cousin came to live with me in Lansdowne. She said she was going to stay until he was out of my head.

I was ashamed that this relationship had been going on for three years. I had been drinking wine daily and smoking weed. My flesh was entertained even if Samson#4BC was not around. I remember my sister and a friend of hers were at my grandmother's house. My sister said, "Rose, Samson#4BC is using you, he is telling everybody in the neighborhood." My sister's friend said he had done the same thing to her and other women.

My response was, "Alright." I kept moving. I did not want to process or hear what they were saying. I was having fun. I had been in and out of the hospital with surgeries, my husband left me. I was going to enjoy this half glass as long as I could. I thought, "Besides, I have the money and the time."

I shared information about Samson#4BC with my aunt. My aunt liked Samson#4BC. He knew how to charm women and make them smile. Samson#4BC was good at having a good time and laughing. My aunt said it was all right to spend money on a man. My mother disagreed with that way of treating a man. My mother did not know my aunt gave me this advice.

I found it was easy to keep Samson#4BC happy. I would purchase cases of beer and he loved hoagies and fast food. I would feed him and watch him get high. Samson#4BC would say, "Wake me up so I can get home in time." I never did.

My cousin from Wilmington would answer my phone and tell him not to call back. I laid in the bed lovesick. I knew my cousin was right and I knew I needed her help. I had become addicted to Samson#4BC. I had forgotten the person I was. I let men humiliate me for so long that I just went along to get along.

I was letting wisdom into my life. I came to myself. I hated Samson#4BC for what I allowed him to do. I took the clothes I bought him and put them into a green plastic bag and went to 52nd & Baltimore Avenue and gave them to a junkie I knew.

My cousin said, "Rose, do you realize that his wife could have sued you for distress in her marriage?" I began to think, "What if they were setting me up?" My finances had to be protected. I became frightened with the thought of a set up. I worked hard on myself to get strong enough to fight off his charms if and when he tried to come back.

Samson#4BC rang my bell at 1:00 am in the morning in the suburbs. Samson#4BC was yelling out my name. I told him to leave; that I was phoning the police. Samson#4BC left. It would be several years before I saw him again. I saw him at a funeral. He spoke and I rolled my eyes. I remembered at that moment when he said my foot looked like it was an elephant's foot, and he laughed. Samson#4BC came over and said, "Can I get a hug?" I barely hugged him and walked away.

I recall Samson#4BC wanting to move in with me permanently. I was considering this move. I phoned my lawyer. I'd heard of situations where wealthy women had to pay a less-than-wealthy man money if their relationship had broken up. I did not want this to happen to me. My lawyer had me to come in to her office. To my surprise, another lawyer who represented me in my divorce was there, as well. Both lawyers warned me to not let him have mail come to my home and definitely do not let him move in. My lawyers then questioned why I was with him in the first place. My mind was changing. I was blessed. The seeds were being planted so by the time I saw my cousin from Wilmington, I was ready to leave the madness.

Samson#5BC

I noticed my maturing and changing was occurring at rapid speed. I loved who I was becoming and recalled the woman I used to be before my accident. I met Samson#5BC during a time when Samson#4BC had gone to be with his baby mommas.

When I met Samson#5BC, I had not moved to the suburbs. I was in the beginning stages of spending the money I had acquired. I had never met anyone like Samson#5BC. He was classy, drug and alcohol free. There was railroad construction happening on our block. The street had been blocked off because of construction. Samson#5BC had a jeep. Samson#5BC looked healthy; he worked out. Samson#5BC reminded me of the men who would speak to me before I had my accident. I was reminded of my flavor and my type. I was excited. Samson#4BC had a beer gut and had no automobile. I was moving up with the male species in spite of my facial injury.

Samson#5BC said there must be a God for you to have lived. I was impressed with that statement. I had a few friends come over. Samson#5BC told me right away, "I would never talk to girls like that. They were too ghetto." Samson#5BC said that I was a better woman than that. He said I would become what I was around. I thought to myself, "They were here with me when no one else could stand to look at me." I liked when Samson#5BC talked. I was learning how to be better. I was learning to think about my future and not just the moment. Samson#5BC talked about school and education. I had purchased some rings from a jewelry store on Woodland Avenue. Samson#5BC asked where I purchased the cheap jewelry. I told him. He asked the price. I said $135.00. Samson#5BC laughed. and said, "I will take you to buy some real jewelry." I said, "Ok."

I asked Samson#5BC, "How much money should I bring?" Samson#5BC said $10,000. I decided to take $20,000 in cash. I saw pictures of famous black basketball stars who made purchases at the store; at least that was the implication. I heard commercials of this store on television and the radio. Once the owner knew I had cash they gave me a seat and brought me refreshments.

I loved the pieces of jewelry I purchased. I saw the difference in the quality of the $135 ring versus a five thousand dollar ring. I was starting to understand the money I had acquired. I noticed that no one looked at me strangely in the store. I was treated royally. This had never happened with the exception of at the lawyer's office.

Samson#5BC was introducing me to my money. I never told anyone with the exception of my ex-husband, what I had. Samson#5BC introduced me to the cell phone. Besides my daughter and I, he and his son had the walkie-talkie looking phones.

I recall when the lawyer gave me the check to give to the trust company. His statement was, "Your life is about to change." I thought, "Thank you, God." I asked, "What do you mean?" The lawyer responded, "Your family is going to change how they feel about you." My response was, "My family is happy about this money." The lawyer was right.

I had surgery on my nose during the time I was in a relationship with Samson#5BC. He rode a motorcycle too; it was nice. Samson#5BC always wore nice gear to match his bike and his leather boots were always fierce. Samson#5BC said that when he put on his helmet he could smell the stench of the blood that came from my nose. He said the smell was all over him.

Samson#5BC spoke about the stench in great length with disgust and cruelty as if I wanted my nose to smell that way. I was embarrassed and ashamed about what he had experienced. I thought, "How many men will criticize me for injuries I did not want or the circumstances that came with them?"

I would always hear my mother's voice when men were cruel to me, saying, "Haven't you had enough men?" Samson#5BC would eventually ask me for money to help him in some venture and to purchase some expensive items. I told him my lawyers put me on a budget and that I no longer had access to thousands as I once had.

I knew the relationship was over after the smell incident. I was embarrassed and ashamed about the smell. Samson#5BC stopped calling shortly after I had no money to share. I was glad for the break. I had money, my teen daughter, family and I was learning about me.

Samson#6BC

I drove my Sec 560 Mercedes to Fairmount Park on the hill where everybody meets. I met Samson#6BC during the summer in Fairmount Park at the spot Wil Smith sings about in "*Summertime.*" I parked my car, blasting the song "*Summertime.*" I had a nice sound system put in my car. I kept it detailed because that's what the brothers said I should do with a Mercedes Benz. My black Benz was waxed and glowing. My leather burgundy interior was shining.

I was feeling like a star in the park the day I met Samson#6BC. My looks did not matter to me that day – my blind eye, the structure of my nose and lips, or my abnormal looking right foot. I was happy. I stepped out of my car and parked next to me was a navy blue Sec 560 Mercedes. I hadn't noticed the car when I parked.

I proceeded to the front of my car when Samson#6BC, looking like Idris Alba, he spoke. He said, "I like your car." I said, "Thank you." He smiled. I grinned and asked, "Is that your car?" Samson#6BC said, "Yes, it's a Benz thing." I said, "Yes it is!"

Samson#6BC walked over to look at my car and we began comparing vehicles. We talked for at least three hours and listened to music from his car. Samson#6BC asked for my number and I gave him both of them. Samson#6BC was impressed that I had a cell phone. He didn't. I thought of Samson#5BC. He had a cell phone.

I liked Samson#6BC – his humor and his style. Samson#5BC had style. I always liked a man who can dress nice – manly nice. Samson#6BC never once said anything about my looks, about my money or the power he felt money brings. I liked going to shows, fancy restaurants and getting dressed up. I paid the way and Samson#6BC came. Eventually Samson#6BC would talk about my money too.

I wanted to forget how I looked and the money helped. I wanted to forget the pain and suffering the burns caused me. I knew I could not hide or avoid my feelings forever. Samson#6BC had a girlfriend who he had a son with. Samson#6BC lived with her and I didn't care. He showed me photos of her and she was beautiful.

I believed that I would only have the half glass. I believed I would never have a committed relationship because of my looks, my scars. I realized, sadly, the women who were involved with the Samsons were not getting trustful men.

Samson#6BC always wanted to sit in my office. He says it was power in that room, because of my finances. My thoughts were that I died, went to hell, was burned physically and came back by the Grace of God for that money, which can never compensate for my loss. I sensed that Samson#6BC hoped he would see some financial paper work in my office, but those papers were securely hidden out of sight.

Samson#6BC's Benz started breaking down. I knew with him not having a job, he would soon ask me for money. He says he collects unemployment. However, his girlfriend works. Samson#6BC did not have a Mercedes Benz engine. He had a Chevy engine.

I thought, "It's not a Benz thing, it's a money thing." I gave Samson#6BC money to fix his car. I knew without his car, he could not come see me. I did not want to be without companionship.

I started getting angry with myself. I knew it was time for a change. My relationship with Samson#6BC ended because his Chevy Engine was going bad and my intention was to help once. I thought, "Those good looks aren't helping me keep my mind together." I was still scheduled for surgeries. I decided one day to stop talking to Samson#6BC, and I did.

I had hoped that my ex-husband would change his mind about our marriage. I heard a Stevie Wonder song called "*Rocket Love*." I felt my ex-husband had done exactly what is being said in the song.

I understand that trauma affects people in ways they never expect. The song, "*Rocket Love*" speaks of how a man longed for a woman since he was born; a woman who is kind. I interpret it as you made me certain you would always be there, you took me on a rocket ship and gave me a star. I know my marriage had tough times but we shared a little bit of heaven. My going through this tragedy somehow caused me to be dropped into this cold, too cold, world. I wouldn't do that to a dog. My ex-husband loved me and left me to be handled by the Samsons who needed help themselves.

I had not been in a relationship since 1991 and I was living just fine. I had decided men were out of my life forever. I had been hurt several times. I felt my looks caused the hurt. My goals were to work on myself, my mind, body and spirit. I had my family, my money and I was building a relationship with my Father in Heaven.

I would read a great deal when I lived at my grandmother's house. I knew I needed to change me now that I intended to keep the ungodly people away from me. I started looking for my Maker to tell me how to live, how to be.

One of my favorite bible verses is Psalms 40:1-4

"I waited patiently for the LORD; he turned to me and heard my cry. 2| He lifted me out of the slimy pit, out of the mud and mire; he set my feet on a rock and gave me a firm place to stand. 3| He put a new song in my mouth, a hymn of praise to our God. Many will see and fear the LORD and put their trust in him. 4| Blessed is the one who trusts in the LORD, who does not look to the proud, to those who turn aside to false gods."

I knew the first four verses were me. I had to learn to be patient even though I cried a lot of days and nights. I was in a pit. I was incarcerated in a body that I did not want. I was stuck in it like trying to get your foot out of a deep puddle of mud.

I diligently kept looking for a place of peace with God. I often sing songs of praise to my Father in Heaven. I sing songs thanking Him for taking care of me in a special way, a way only a Father would know how to care for their child. My voice will praise His name.

I put my trust in the Lord. There was no one who could remove my hurt but God. My lifestyle changed. I was praying all the time. I was talking to God. I was listening for the Holy Spirit's direction. I was stepping out on faith. My time was spent at church, with family and in the gym. I had obtained structure and a routine that I would follow forever.

I decided to start a non-profit organization in 2005. My support group meeting had ended one evening. I was loading my car with materials from the meeting. My mother and sister, along with several people, were standing near my car. A strange car comes up with someone I had not seen since my teen years. My sister knew him right away. I am introduced to Samson#7AC by my sister.

Samson#7AC

I remembered Samson#7AC. We greeted one another and I turned to speak to someone else. I noticed that Samson#7AC was still standing near me and staring. Samson#7AC said, "I'd like to take you to dinner." I said, "Dinner? No thank you." I know we had a childhood together, but I don't know this man.

I gave him literature about my organization with my business/cell number after he asked if he could call. Samson#7AC was not appealing to me, but he was kind. I went to lunch with Samson#7AC and soon after, he attended many support group meetings. I am amazed how my feelings for Samson#7AC developed.

My daddy and I would bop (a dance) to the Isley Brothers *"This Old Heart of Mine."* I always felt the words of this song were how my daddy felt about my mother. I remember dancing with Daddy on Friday and Saturday nights. My daddy would play this song over and over and we would dance until exhaustion.

As I recall past relationships with the diverse situations and my immaturity, I recall the words of the song *"This Old Heart of Mine."* The words are a reminder of how I have felt in my past relationships.

My heart has been broken a thousand times and each time I am in a relationship, when it's time to say good night, I think the person will never return.

I think because I show the love I feel, I am sometimes taken advantage of. My heart is weak for those I have loved. Like the song says, I try to hide the hurt I feel inside but this old heart of mine keeps me messed up in my head. I feel no matter how many times you leave, I will take you back.

I loved this song because of the times I danced with my daddy. At times, I wonder if it's because of this song that I would tolerate trying to love a man. My new song is, *"I Am a Big Girl Now, no more Daddy's little girl,"* by the Stylistics.

Samson#7AC would take me to the movies, buy me gifts, and take me to dinner. Samson#7AC would buy food for the times he would stay with me. Samson#7AC never gave me any money for myself and I never asked.

My birthday came and Samson#7AC gave me the best birthday in years. My ex-husband always did great things for my birthday. Samson#7AC bought cake, a lovely watch, a card and took me out to dinner. I was appreciative. Someone was buying for me for a change.

I would explain my spiritual connection with God to Samson#7AC.

I knew I would not be able to continue the relationship with Samson#7AC. I enjoyed what Samson#7AC was bringing into my life. He could feed my flesh but he had nothing for my spirit. I needed a Samson who loved God and I knew he would not be perfect. I need and want a man to worship God with me. Samson#7AC appealed to me because of his intellect and his political knowledge.

Samson#7AC lacked discipline when it came to his health, but more importantly, I saw no relationship with God. I had trust issues because of his work schedule and he liked going to the casinos. Samson#7AC would methodically chip at my confidence.

I saw patterns beginning to formulate. The more affection I gave, the more he became mean. Because of his variety of medical issues and his job, it affected his personality. I saw character problems. Samson#7AC never married and he said none of his relationships ever lasted more than 9 months.

I began to become frightened because I knew I was called to a higher standard of spirituality and morality. Samson#7AC never understood and really didn't care to hear about my pain of overcoming. I want the man who loves me or says he loves me to know the traumatic experiences that God brought me through and I want to know his.

My relationship with Samson#7AC lasted 9 months, the length he said his relationships lasted. I ended the relationship. I was broken-hearted. I purposely stayed away from men to avoid hurt because my belief was that I am not a man's first choice. However, I want to feel and know that Samson knows he made a great choice. I did not feel that way with Samson#7AC.

I did know that Samson#7AC was a better man than my before Christ Samsons. My self-esteem and my knowledge of who Christ says I am makes a better me, therefore bringing a better Samson. I questioned myself about which is the better Samson. It's all perspective.

My life improved after I understood that I was no longer angry with my ex-husband, or the Samsons before Christ or Samson#7AC. I sought God more diligently after Samson#7AC. I worked on loving me because none of the Samsons could treat me that well.

I learned it was my responsibility to investigate and date the Samsons before I allowed them into my personal space. I thought about the things that l liked about Samson#7AC. I decided to purchase updated technology and go back to school. Samson#7AC was always reading and learning. I liked that.

I never recalled Samson#7AC saying anything negative about my looks. I do recall Samson#7AC saying, as he was looking into my blessed eye, "I see you, Rose."

I learned from psychology class at Drexel University "Critical Thinking." My Bishop at Bethany Baptist Church taught Critical Thinking. I loved this topic because for too long I have been an emotional thinker. I changed my thinking. I made a decision to position myself for greater things in life. I needed critical thinking and the Holy Ghost to protect me from the evils of the world.

Samson#8AC

I had not noticed how many years it had been since I was in a relationship with a man until the conversation changed with Samson#8AC. I counted those years. It was eight. I laughed remembering I have said many times if I can be married for five good years versus thirty bad years of marriage, I'd take the five.

I went to elementary school with him. I connected with Samson#8AC on Facebook. Samson#8AC and I spoke of growing up in elementary school and where our lives had taken us. We shared some of our life experiences, the good, the sad, the mistakes, and regrets. We talked about what we had learned from our lives.

Samson#8AC phoned me one day and shared his financial problems. I responded by saying, "You are handling." I said, "You have a great job. God has kept and helped you." Samson#8AC said, "God has, but people didn't." I thought to myself I could use his paycheck. Samson#8AC worked professionally making two hundred thousand a year; this is what he said.

I do know the economy for people can change, overspending, taxes and automobiles. etc. Samson#8AC phoned the following day and apologized for his sad moments when he shared his financial situation. I said, "No problem. I may share mine with you."

Samson#8AC had a lust spirit and had previously participated in sex groups. I didn't even know groups existed like this. I had forgotten. Those types of conversations are not the norm for me. Samson#8AC expressed a bitterness about relationships he'd had in the past. I thought to myself, "Wow, he has not forgiven those who hurt him." I saw a pattern of deceit, manipulation and boasting of conquering women.

Samson#8AC thrilled me with the things he knew and the people he knew and met. He knew authors, famous professors and singers. I thought he was fascinating in all areas. I thought to myself, "What a good friend to have." Samson#8AC switched the conversation with flattery. He said he was proud of the things I was doing with Healed With Scars, but he never watched any of my videos or commented on my web page. I was certain he would give me some pointers on updating it. Samson#8AC told me about women he dated that were or could be considered physically disabled.

I never considered myself physically disabled, but of course hindsight, right. I thought Samson#8AC was smarter than Samson#7AC. They both preyed on women who are rarely involved with men. Samson#8AC and Samson#7AC liked spiritual women and women who have some physical handicap.

Samson#7AC dated women who had low self-esteem, obese, jobless or bipolar. Neither of the Samsons was slender, nor healthy or good-looking. They were all right. Their finances appeared to be all right. I thought Samson#8AC was a bitter man.

I know the Holy Spirit was saying to me, "Stop conversing with Samson#8AC, and get out now." My flesh was saying, "Can I play for a little while? It feels and sounds good." I stayed and played.

Both Samsons#7AC and #8AC would verbally attack the ministers of the Gospel right away when I stated a relationship cannot work because we are unequally yoked. Immediately, their response would be, the minister has another woman, homosexual or taking money.

My thought is, "Look who's talking." Samson#7AC & 8AC aspire and do what they are accusing the men of God of doing. I mentioned Steve Harvey's efforts in helping women and they both were negative towards him also. I am thankful for the men of God who warn us, and Steve Harvey's efforts. Sadly, often it takes men to tell women about the manipulation that men use against us and then we listen.

Samson#8AC phoned me every day early in the morning. I liked the attention. Samson#8AC said if we did not get together that years from now I would regret it. I said you are right, I would regret it. I would regret it but the hard lesson would never be forgotten. I made the visit to Samson#8AC. I had never felt so ignored since my ex-husband could not stand to look at me.

I prayed to God, "I know you told me not to come. But, please don't let this man kill me." Samson#8AC's demeanor would change in a second. I knew it must be how I look. Samson#8AC would change back for a few hours and be kind. He would then change to mean and withdrawn. I thought, "Maybe it's not me or how I look." I was scared.

Samson#8AC said, "No one should ever know that I came to visit him. I told him he did not have to worry about that." I would never tell anyone how humiliated I had been treated. I didn't tell him that. I think somehow he knew. Samson#8AC asked me how did I think my visit was. I held my head down. I told him at first when I arrived, he was a little rough, but then he got better. Hell no, he didn't.

I came home and thanked God I was not abused physically. I was abused emotionally. I knew critical thinking and not my emotions had to process my visit. I knew I had to pray for Samson#8AC. I never spoke to him again.

My flesh just wanted to be treated kindly, beautifully like Samson#8AC had done on the phone. How did I miss the signals? I didn't miss the signals. I saw them and ignored them. My goal was to seek and have fun.

Samson#8AC taught me what my Bishop has been saying for years, it starts with a conversation. I phoned Samson#7AC when I got home. My ego and confidence took a hit. My flesh needed or wanted a man to fix what Samson#8AC had broken. I opened up a door with Samson#7AC that I prayed for God to help me get over. I thought I could handle it. I found in a few days Samson#7AC was acting crazy like Samson#8AC. I knew I had to stop this roller coaster ride.

I had hoped to be friends with Samson#7AC but my reason for calling him was to satisfy a hurt. I shut it down with Samson#7AC. He was angry. I am amazed how much alike they are. I have learned that the Samsons that I allowed into my life had hopes and dreams for themselves. I was never included in any plans. I was a come along for their desires.

All the Samsons

My finances blessed me. My comfortable lifestyle blessed a few Samsons. Samsons wanted my lifestyle and not me. I know the Samsons wanted what I obtained through suffering through fire and pain. I know having me act like a wife was included.

My ex-husband was willing to come back for equal access to my money, but I had already been under his leadership and I saw no change in his thinking. I was allowing God to enter my mind and life. My ex-husband said nothing about God.

Samson in the bible was disobedient to God on many occasions. Samson had a lust problem and he was a man of God. He was chosen by God. Judges 13:5 KJV "For, lo, thou shalt conceive, and bear a son; and no razor shall come on his head: for the child shall be a Nazarite unto God from the womb: and he shall begin to deliver Israel out of the hand of the Philistines."

Samson was strong in his physical strength but it did not help the weak areas in his life. God used Samson in spite of his mistakes and God has used us in spite of ours. I am guilty of being disobedient to the Holy Spirit and the ways of God. I thank God for repentance and His love.

I know the struggle people with handicaps, sickness and facial disfigurement suffer. I learned through traumatic events, love from family and friends can protect people from those who seek to take advantage of us. I was provided evidence and signs that said do not get involved with these men. I felt I needed someone to hold, hug me and say they were proud of me for not giving up. My ex-husband or my mother never did. Neither did any of the Samsons. I told everybody, I desired that. My daughter would tell me many times. I am thankful for her acknowledgement.

I remember my mother making two important statements to me. I only wish she were repetitive. My mother said I was a fool if I thought anybody would care or be sympathetic about how I looked. My mom made this statement after white men in a car were yelling evil things to me. My mother's second important statement was, "Haven't you had enough men in your life already?" I said, "Mom, I am in my early thirties." I translated my mother's statement later as being one of concern. My translation: Rose the men that come into your life will only hurt you and use you. My mother was right in 1990.

I believe if there is a possibility of a husband on my journey of life; our foundation must be built on a Godly commitment. Pastor Nicholas Smith of Bethany Baptist Church said this in reference to relationships, "Godly commitment must be the foundation of intimacy. A commitment founded on intimacy is doomed to failure and deceit." Pastor Nicholas Smith also said, "The bible asks two important

116

questions. Who can find a faithful man? Who can find a virtuous woman? Obviously, we can't. If we could, our past relationship choices would have been better. The lesson is, let God work the connecting out. He created the faithful man and the virtuous woman. So, he knows how to find them for you."

I am thankful for the Samsons that I allowed in my life. I have learned my lessons. My thought is to let God do the connecting. I will work on controlling my flesh desires and weaknesses. I am amazed at the pattern and similarities of the Samsons that I had relationships with. The familiar spirit from the first Samson led to the same spirit that attracted me to the similar Samson.

Samson#1BC & 2BC were both incarcerated, seeking money

Samson#3BC & 4BC were both drug users, seeking money

Samson#5BC & 6BC were both seeking money, both well-dressed and good-looking, physically fit

Samson#7AC & 8AC were intellectually stimulating, obese, illnesses caused by obesity, seeking money

I find it humiliating, sad that any person would negatively describe a burn survivor's scars or say negative things about a burn survivor knowing the endurance of pain that has been suffered. I know it is my job to take care of myself. I cannot expect people who are hurting themselves to care for me if they have not dealt with their pain.

The Men of My Youth

My thoughts of Woodland Avenue, the primary street in the area where I lived, were there could never be a place better to live. I walked from 63rd & Woodland Avenue to 43rd & Woodland Avenue from age eleven to eighteen years old. My friends or siblings accompanied me during some of those walks.

I played with friends in the area from 50th to 46th and Woodland Avenue. In the 1960's to 1974, the avenue appeared prosperous. I recall small bars on the avenue; a supermarket, a State Store (where wine and liquor was sold), a few small grocery stores, SEPTA (Southeastern Pennsylvania Transportation Authority) was called PTC (Public Transportation Company), green was the color for the trollies and buses. What we now know as Citizens Bank was called PSFS (Philadelphia Savings Fund Society). The police cars were red. There were telephone booths on most corners and cell phones were non-existent.

My neighborhood was on Woodland Avenue with the small streets that surrounded it. I never thought that Woodland Avenue would mean so much to me until after leaving it in 1975.

I never thought that memories of the men in my pre-teen and teenage life would matter. I am happy for those young men of my youth who said such nice things to me.

My memories of my youth were of guys wanting me and saying I am pretty. My father and the men in the family said that I was cute. My family would say who I looked like. My parents and their relatives were known for their good looks.

I grew up in my pre-teens and teenage years where the environment I lived in was based on if you could fight, dance or were pretty. I grew up in the time of the Cooley High movie, 1975. I thought of money, when the summertime came to get a summer job, when a party cost a $1 to get in, or money for school. I must not omit when my parents were arguing about money and bills.

I thank those brothers in my youth, because programmed in my thoughts were their compliments. I think of the young men I thought were fine and cool. If those brothers said it, it held a truth.

I recall a prominent OG (Old Gangster), or my old head. My old head had a reputation for being a good fighter, good dancer, good-looking, cool, smart and making money. I was fourteen when he said, "When you grow up, you will be a great woman." I never forgot what he said.

My transition back to the Woodland Avenue area resulted in me living with my mother because of my injuries from the automobile fire. Many people reached out to me in the first couple of weeks of my return, as did my old head.

My conversation with my old head was encouraging. I am still amazed how a man can speak into your life and it can break you or make you. I tell women all the time to be careful what man you listen to.

I have a great relationship with my OG now. He is a Christian a man of God. I was able to end and understand my last relationships with Samson#7AC and #8AC because of my OG's wisdom. My OG's first question to me was if these men were saved. I said no. I confessed Samson#7AC and #8AC were rejected by me in my teenage years.

I shared everything with my OG and he responded to the nonsense that I was blinded by. My OG helped with my ego and my critical thinking. I was coming out of the mess, no doubt, because my peace was at stake.

My family's responses to my looks are also programed in my thoughts. Since my elementary school days, my family has been telling me that I was pretty. I was told my gap in my teeth made my smile nice. My hair was a nice length and I grew into a nice looking teenager and young lady. I attended modeling school, Barbizon Modeling School, on Walnut Street in Philadelphia when I was seventeen through eighteen. I modeled at the Bellevue Stratford Hotel on Broad Street; it was our graduation ceremony. I modeled two outfits and was chosen to be first to walk on the runway. I purchased an outfit from New York to assure myself I would be wearing something unique.

My response to negative statements since I've been facially burned with scars was hard to process in the beginning of my accepting my new face. My inner person kept thinking, "Why do people say I look horrible?" My life for twenty years plus was not used to being rejected because of my looks.

My discussion with myself would take years of understanding how I should process others' responses to my looks versus my thoughts of how I look to myself. I thought of myself as beautiful even more so after my relationship with God matured. God tells me who I am. I am wonderfully made. I am God's child. How can I hold my head down?

I've read Proverbs 31 many times and it never speaks about the wife's appearance or how she should look physically. Proverbs 31 speaks of the virtuous woman's wisdom, skills and compassion that come from her reverence of God. The Proverbs 31 wife's attractiveness radiates from her character.

On occasions when I see a man from my youth, he gives me a compliment about my strength and perseverance. I want to say thank you to all the men of my youth who liked and loved me for my looks. I want to thank you for all the positive compliments with or without a motive.

I recall showing a young lady in church a photo of how I used to look. I don't recall what led me to show her the photo. The young lady said, "Ms. Rose, you were cute and you would have had a lot of men wanting you." I said, "Thank you for saying I was cute." I never responded about the men wanting me. My thought about her was, she herself is physically beautiful. I was sure she knew about men wanting a good-looking woman.

I thank God for my memories. I am thankful for the men that compliment my strength and my inner beauty. I have learned that faithfulness to God creates the inner beauty that shows up on the physical body. I have learned that a beautiful face is desired by men. I am thankful for the years of my beauty. I am thankful that I experienced marriage in its good and bad. I am thankful for true loves I have had in my life. I realize that some people will never have what I have had.

I am thankful for when sickness, unfortunate life situations, and no physical beauty, transitioned me to a lonely place that God, maturity and critical thinking were here to contribute to sustaining my new life.

The Photo by the Lake

I stood on the bank of the Cayuga Lake, Ithaca, New York. I stood there knowing I had disobeyed God by coming to New York. I had gone to New York with the wrong intentions. I had gone to be with a male friend who said it didn't matter what I looked like, but when I got there, I was greeted at the train station with a cold stare as if I were an alien. I felt like my soul ran from me to hide.

I was frozen in place as I stood on the bank of the Cayuga Lake. My thoughts did not rush for processing. I thought carefully one thought at a time. My sense of time was zero. Time seemed to stand still. I heard the waters rushing to the bank as I stood unable to move.

I had been to Bermuda, Jamaica, and Germany and could not recall ever seeing a lake, land, mountain and a clear blue sky connected together as if it were sewn with an invisible thread coming together like a patched quilt. I admired each creation made by God. I thought, "I am standing on dirt, land and grass God made." I have stood on dirt, land and grass before but this was a spiritual moment captured in a photo helping me to retain a memory of a moment.

I looked at the water and a breeze came by, the wind. My hair is blowing in the wind. I am reminded of Stevie Wonder's song the *Answer My Friend Is Blowin' in the Wind*. I watched the water move back and forth making gentle, but strong, waves. I thought if the water had been blue, I might have fainted in the moment of God's awesomeness. I now believe the wind was God touching me, saying you'll be safe in this strange land I have traveled to. I never understood Stevie's song as a child. How could an answer blow in the wind? I know the answer blowing in the wind is God, my Father in Heaven. God is the answer to everything!

I looked at the mountain so close to me, but yet it was afar. I thought how awesome to create a mountain to oversee the lake and the land. I thought how amazing the mountain looks as if it touches the sky. I looked at the sky like I never have before. It was marvelous. I tried to imagine God's view looking at His sky, His Mountain, His Lake, His land and me. I, too, am a creation of the Creator, mind-blowing.

I knew along with the message of reassuring my safety, God's Genesis story of Creation came to my mind. I know we need faith to understand all of God's creations and His ways. I stood at the bank knowing that I meant something to God. I know regardless of my trials and stressful times God gives me something to smile, laugh and to be grateful for. I knew standing on the bank of the Cayuga Lake, Ithaca, New York, at that moment, my God is real.

I thought as I was looking at the photo and listening to the words of "*Blowin' in the Wind*" – how it speaks of man, a white dove (Holy Spirt), a mountain, the sea and the wind. "*Blowin' in the Wind*" was released in 1966 and the same issues Stevie Wonder sang about in 1966 are still the issues we as a human race face today.

Living My Journey

I have lived through a trauma. Wow, unbelievable what I have come through. I have been traumatized. I have had the bodily injury, the wounds and the shock. I have the painful emotional experience. I have been traumatized.

I wanted to read the definition of trauma, it is defined (medically) as a bodily injury, wound, or shock; (psychiatry) a painful emotional experience or shock, often producing a lasting psychic effect and sometimes, a neurosis. I am trauma.

My thirty years of living through this trauma has been to prove to my family and the public that I am sane, capable and all right. My hardest fight was believing I was loved when I felt rejected. I was rejected, but I denied it because emotionally that hurt worse than the burn wounds. I took the "pretend love" from the wrong people and it broke me, it hurt me.

My peace is the state of mind that I will war to keep. I understand that stresses that I have no control over will come. I will oversee my thoughts, my actions and my relationships to maintain a peaceful state of mind even when crazy is happening around me. My peace is my position of power.

I received a coupon from Chick-Fil-A for a free chicken sandwich. I was hungry, but it was dark outside. I looked at the time it said 3:45 p.m. I thought, "It's rush hour time and a storm is coming." I have a saying that food will get you in trouble. My thought is if I cannot control my flesh from food, I can find myself in trouble. I wanted the sandwich. I paused and thought about the storm and the distance to the Chick-Fil-A. I decided I would go and take my time. I began my drive and a drizzle of rain started. I am in trouble because the storm has come. Rain is pouring. I can hardly see. I put on my warning lights so, hopefully, whoever is behind me can see my flashing red lights.

I prayed, "Lord, I did not control my flesh and now I am in a storm." I know a revelation will be revealed. I prayed, "Lord, keep me safe." I could not see the road but I knew the streets that led to Chick-Fil-A. Cars were pulling over to the side of the road. I wondered, "Should I pull over? I can see nothing in front of me." I drove slowly. I asked, "Father in Heaven, should I pull over?" I felt peace, and the Holy Spirit said, "Do not stop." I proceeded for a few minutes, the rain stopped and the sun was shining bright. I said, "God you are awesome. Thank you."

My revelation when I decided to go into a storm was to call on God, He will answer and make a way. I learned that a storm does not last forever and that the light of God will be waiting for you. I went into the restaurant and got my free sandwich. I decided to take it home to eat.

I proceeded the same way I came and, wow, there's the storm again. I knew another revelation would be revealed. I continued to drive and it was hard to see again. I have my warning signals flashing. I see the same cars stopped on the road that I passed earlier. I continue on my way home. I gave God praise when I arrived home and it was still pouring rain. My revelation was another storm would come. God gave me a revelation, seek Him in all storms, keep moving and work my faith in Him. I had peace through the storm again.

I recall a song Shirley Murdock sings, *As We Lay.* The song is about a man and a woman who are married to other people who spend the night together. She sings we can't turn back the hand of time, we shared each other, as we lay we forgot about tomorrow and the price we have to pay. She sings, in the morning the reality is we go our separate ways, we forgot about the pain we'll cause. She continues to sing that we should have counted the cost, but we got lost in the seconds, in the minutes. Whether this song is true or not, it's an example of how peace can be given up and others are hurt for hours of fornication and/or pleasure.

I talked about the Samsons (men) that were once in my life. I did not express how deep those hurts were or how long it took me to get them out of my head, my thoughts. I know the Samsons I met before turning my life over to Christ left me with nothing to hope for, just left me feeling foolish, seeking another lust-filled relationship and the consequences of men that come to play.

I suffered consequences with the Samsons who came into my life after turning my life over to Christ, but I had hope in Christ. I knew after repentance, my destiny and purpose were still valid. Hallelujah! I also know I do not like giving up my peace. I gave up my peace for some fleshly fun. I gave up my position of power, my peace.

I recall the times I have neglected to fight for my peace. I neglected to spend time with God. I would spend time with God on the run, while I was doing other things. I thought if I played gospel songs in my car and in my home that may be enough to sustain me, to convince God and me that we had a relationship.

I thought praising God throughout the day when something good happened was enough. I found it was not enough for my relationship with God. I do believe that the acknowledgments I listed are good, I was thinking of Him.

My spirit knew I needed more to sustain me. I had to stop moving and sit down with my Father. I needed to put my complete focus on Him. I wanted to visit with God. I needed to thank God, speak to God, and listen to God. I came to realize I love God more than to share a microwave visit with my Father.

I recalled when I would visit my grandmother. I thought it was a visit. I looked up the word visit; "to go or come to see (someone) out

127

of friendship or for social reasons. 2. to stay with as a guest for a time." In the nice weather, my grandmother would sit on her porch with her beads, earrings, bracelet, with red lipstick, her hair done and her beautiful eyes. I thought how lovely she was.

I would run onto the porch and say, "Hi Grandmom. I am thirsty or I need to go to the bathroom. Then I would come back to the porch where she is sitting, say how pretty she looked and say, "See you later."

My grandmother spoke to me about my not visiting her. I responded, "Grandmom, I do. I saw you the other day when I came to go to the bathroom." My grandmother said, "That is not a visit." She said I did not sit down and spend any time with her. I understood what my grandmother was saying. There was no value, nor any time spent with her. I can visit a doctor, a clothing store, a restaurant and spend more time there than I had spent with my grandmother. I started sitting down and talking for hours with my grandmother. I am so glad she taught me what it is to visit.

My position of peace comes from visiting with God, spending time with Him. I learn patience and discipline when I sit and visit with my Father. God teaches me when I sit still and think of Him ONLY.

I no longer jeopardize my peace. I must war for my peace. I know maintaining my peace depends on me knowing who I am. I am a child of God. I attend to my spiritual life daily. Throughout the day, I talk with God and listen to God. I assemble with other Christians and witness about God's love and His Son, Jesus.

For my physical life, I take the time to rest, eat right to live healthy, exercise to live healthy and visit the doctors on scheduled visits.

[John 14:27 NIV] 27 "Peace I leave with you; my peace I give you. I do not give to you as the world gives. Do not let your hearts be troubled and do not be afraid."

[John 15:9-10 NIV] 9 "As the Father has loved me, so have I loved you. Now remain in my love.
10 If you keep my commands, you will remain in my love, just as I have kept my Father's commands and remain in his love."

I started Healed With Scars, "an organization for people with burn injury," in 2005. I did not want to start a group for burn survivors. I had been part of several burn camps for children and young adults. My experience from the burn camps was confusing. I found the burn camps to be sympathetic and empathetic for the children. I was confused because there was no preparation for the children returning home. For an entire week, they were catered to, spoiled and fussed over. I loved seeing the children so happy. It hurt to see them hurting and crying when they got on the bus to return home. Most of the children were returning home to abusive and economically poor homes.

I had culture shock as an adult. For a week, I was not concerned about wearing makeup, or people staring because of my burns. Everyone was able to be themselves minus the scars, with the exception of some who were on pain meds and those who needed their bandages changed. I saw that even with the medical problems, there was a freedom we all shared. No one laughed about our scars or spoke negatively against us because of our burn scars. I often thought about starting a program for children with burn injuries.

I started to feel like I was the only person in Philadelphia who had facial burns. I needed to see other adults who had suffered facial burns. I wanted to start a support group for adults. I had doubts and fears. I saw a minister on television and now he is my pastor, Bishop David G. Evans. Bishop wrote a book titled *"Healed Without Scars."* I bought and I read his book. I was spirit-led to call an organization that I had not yet started Healed With Scars.

I am glad and proud to say that Healed With Scars is a 501 c-3, the only support group of this kind in the city of Philadelphia and has served the burn community for ten years. I will be the first to say Healed With Scars has helped me. I felt alone in a society that was not accepting of facial scarring.

I am thankful for the uncomfortable feelings the Holy Spirit kept sending me until I took action. I am glad that people with burn injuries have been blessed because of Healed With Scars.

In the Bible, Paul told the people of Thessalonica to work hard and live a quiet life, mind their own business. I have decided to live this way.

> [1Th 4:11-12 NIV] 11 "and to make it your ambition to lead a quiet life: You should mind your own business and work with your hands, just as we told you,
> 12 so that your daily life may win the respect of outsiders and so that you will not be dependent on anybody."

I am working with women with and without burn injuries who have been hurt by making wrong decisions with men, and women who have been manipulated by men. I believe that men are to lead, protect, teach, love and care for women. I believe men should be taught how to lead a wife, children and not treat them like a squad or sports team, getting rid of people when they no longer benefit a team. I believe that women should not play the role of a wife to a man who isn't a husband to them.

I respect a song Aretha Franklin sings, titled "*A Rose is Still a Rose*." The song is about a girl who had sex with a man who pretended to like her and the consequences she suffers after he leaves her. Paul writes to Thessalonica telling the people how they should live.

[1Th 4:3-8 NIV] 3 "It is God's will that you should be sanctified: that you should avoid sexual immorality;
4 that each of you should learn to control your own body in a way that is holy and honorable,
5 not in passionate lust like the pagans, who do not know God;

6 and that in this matter no one should wrong or take advantage of a brother or sister. The Lord will punish all those who commit such sins, as we told you and warned you before.
7 For God did not call us to be impure, but to live a holy life.
8 Therefore, anyone who rejects this instruction does not reject a human being but God, the very God who gives you his Holy Spirit."

My Father in Heaven has delivered me from many of the situations that I caused and others I did not. I have done it the world's way and found myself in situations and places that have caused me to suffer.

I know God's way. I know when things in life go wrong that I have a relationship with my Father who can make things right. I believe God. I believe His Word.

[1Th 5:2-8 NIV] 2 "for you know very well that the day of the Lord will come like a thief in the night.
3 While people are saying, "Peace and safety," destruction will come on them suddenly, as labor pains on a pregnant woman, and they will not escape.
4 But you, brothers and sisters, are not in darkness so that this day should surprise you like a thief.
5 You are all children of the light and children of the day. We do not belong to the night or to the darkness.
6 So then, let us not be like others, who are asleep, but let us be awake and sober.
7 For those who sleep, sleep at night, and those who get drunk, get drunk at night.
8 But since we belong to the day, let us be sober, putting on faith and love as a breastplate, and the hope of salvation as a helmet."

I know a Christian woman who lives in Georgia. I admire this woman. I have had the pleasure of looking into her life. She has shared her Christian walk. This woman plants flowers in her yard and around her home. I receive pleasure when she sends me pictures of the planting, tending and reaping. I was walking near my home and thought of the Georgia woman's pretty, colorful flowers, and I smiled. I realized that the way she tends to her flowers is the way she lives her life and the way I live mine. I smiled.

I know there are times when she has to buy products to assist her with her planting and maintenance. Other people are involved for this to happen. We both go to church. Church is where we receive maintenance for our relationship with God. Other people are involved, pastors, believers and teachers, etc. Church gives us the opportunity to praise God together with other believers. Once we receive our maintenance, we go home and continue to live our lives with God.

The woman of God in Georgia described to me how she gets rid of the weeds, things that hinder the growth of her flowers. She explained the watering, the tending and that some flowers can choke other flowers; therefore those flowers are not planted.

I decided my relationship with God would not be hindered. Whatever and whomever interferes will be removed. I understand that I decide who enters my space. I received a suggestion or a tip from the woman of God in Georgia. She said all flowers cannot be planted together, for some flowers choke the others. I will not allow myself to be choked by trying to force relationships.

I have been rejected by people, men and women, because of my facial looks. I would try to please and do whatever I could to make it work. I not only choked myself, I was choking others by trying to force relationships.

My face has gone through many physical changes and I was not always easy to look at or be around. I admire nurses and doctors who can bear to look at physical injuries and help heal them.

I smile when I think of God. He is real. Thinking of those pretty flowers had me smiling about God and my friend's Christian walk. Paul said work with your hands and mind your own business. This is how she lives. I am glad to have met the woman of God from Georgia and other Christians whose lives reflect the scriptures in 1st Thessalonians 4: 11-12, 4: 3-8, 5: 2-8.

I am inspired by a statement my Georgia friend uses in describing living a quiet life, "a part of everything, but yet NOTHING." I translate this statement to do the work of the Lord, live in the world but NOTHING of the world has me or controls me. I know I do things to maintain my relationship with my Father, but I also know He does things for our relationship too. I am God's child and He tends to me. I am THANKFUL.

[Rom 1:16-17 NIV] 16 "For I am not ashamed of the gospel, because it is the power of God that brings salvation to everyone who believes: first to the Jew, then to the Gentile.
17 For in the gospel the righteousness of God is revealed--a righteousness that is by faith from first to last, just as it is written: 'The righteous will live by faith.'"

About the Author

Rosemary Worthy-Washington was born and educated in Philadelphia, PA. She graduated from Edward Bok Vocational High School where she studied shorthand and typing. Additionally, she studied at Community College of Philadelphia and Drexel University. Rosemary enlisted in the United States Army in 1976 where she traveled to Stuttgart, Germany.

Rosemary's life would transition in a way no one who knew her expected. She suffered through a nearly fatal automobile accident on Wednesday, January 8, 1986 on Chamounix Drive, located in Fairmount Park, Philadelphia, PA. Rosemary does not recall or remember the accident.

Rosemary's car was struck by a passenger van; her car hit a tree and exploded. The driver of the van died in the collision. Rosemary was thrown from her car while she was engulfed in flames. She was burned on her face, her head, and her legs. She suffered 1st, 2nd and 3rd degree burns, broken legs and a concussion.

Rosemary, also known as Rose, endured the severe pain burns cause and endured over a hundred surgeries. She would learn to walk again and learn how to live with one eye. She was challenged with infections and surgeries that failed. Her emotional, mental, physical, financial and relationship stability was challenged daily in the early years as she learned to accept the changes of her multiplicity of faces. She referred to herself as the "Woman with Many Faces."

135

Rosemary's faith would give her strength to overcome many obstacles. She says her faith in her Lord and Savior, Jesus, guided her through all of her challenges.

Rosemary started Healed With Scars, "an organization for people with burn injury" in 2005. She participated in and completed two half marathons, one for Jefferson Hospital in 1999 and the 2015 Hot Chocolate 15K for the Ronald McDonald House Charities. She has had articles written about her and Healed With Scars in the *Courier Post* and a local paper, the *Anointed News Journal*. She has been interviewed on KYW News Radio by Lynne Adkins. Cherry Hill Health and Racquetball Club featured her in a video. She was featured on a television show called *Soul Survivors,* and is a frequent guest on *Let's Talk Safety* with the Philadelphia Fire Commissioners' past, Lloyd Ayers and present, Derrick Sawyer. Additionally, she was a guest on *Freedom of Fire*, LaSalle TV where she discussed Healed With Scars with Philadelphia Fire Commissioner, Derrick Sawyer.

Rosemary was an honoree and recipient of the "Circle of Winners" where she received a trophy presented by the *Anointed News Journal*. Rosemary is most proud of receiving a plaque presented by the Women to Women Ministries of Bethany Baptist Church, The Women of Excellence Award, "For Encouragement, Inspiration and Motivation to Women."

Rosemary has two favorite movies that have encouraged her journey in serving others, *"The Razor's Edge"* and the *"Song of Bernadette."* She says both of the main characters in these movies accepted that their revelation for their lives is to serve others, and to continue to seek, love and honor God. Rosemary has accepted her revelation about her life to serve others, and to continue to seek, love and honor God.

Rosemary attended Bethel Deliverance International Church located in Wyncote, PA and pastored by Bishop Eric Lambert. She attended this church for 10 years. Rosemary has a married daughter and two grandchildren. Rosemary moved from Southwest Philadelphia and now lives in Cherry Hill, NJ, where she attends Bethany Baptist Church in Lindenwold, NJ where Bishop David Evans is the pastor.

Follow Rose on Facebook at:
https://www.facebook.com/IWillNotBeAshamed?fref=ts

Communicate with Rose via email at:
ExposedIAmNotAshamed@gmail.com

Learn more about Healed With Scars at
http://www.healedwithscars.org/

Made in the USA
Charleston, SC
17 September 2015